wooden houses

wooden houses

from log cabins to beach houses

Judith Miller

photography by **James Merrell**

RYLAND
PETERS
& SMALL

LONDON NEW YORK

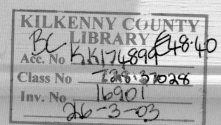
First published in Great Britain in
1997 by Ryland Peters & Small
Cavendish House
51–55 Mortimer Street
London W1N 7TD
Text copyright © Judith Miller 1997
Design and photographs copyright ©
Ryland Peters & Small 1997

10 9 8 7 6 5 4 3

Designer Paul Tilby

Editor Zia Mattocks

Senior Editor Sian Parkhouse

Contributors John Wainwright and
Lynn Bryan

Production Kate Mackillop

Art Director Jacqui Small

Publishing Director Anne Ryland

Contents

Foreword

The Nature of Wood

Wood has a quality that can be matched by no other building material, adding an extra dimension to its surroundings and exhibiting a unique combination of colour, form and texture. It offers a good compromise between strength and flexibility, and performs well under both compression and tension. As such, it is well suited not only for making up the structural components of a building frame, but also for use in floors, stairs, panelling, windows, doors and furniture. When natural wood is treated with wax polish, wood stain or varnish, the beauty of the grain is a thing of wonder. In a room where the walls, floor, door, window frames, chairs and tables are made of wood, the various subtleties of colour, light and shade create an amazing array of visual effects.

In forested countries, building with wood is a tradition and often the only method of construction. Drawing from this wealth of experience, modern-day architecture students learn about the properties of wood – the ways it is cut, the difference between milled and hand-sawn timber, how it is dried, the effects of sun and other weathering, which type is best for exteriors and which for interiors – and how they can use these unique characteristics to enhance any structure they design and build. Many aspects of contemporary wooden-house design have been shaped by the dwellings of our ancestors, whose lifestyles and pastimes are revealed by their legacy of craftsmanship. In turn, modern society will also leave traces of the ways in which imaginations have been stretched, with a fusion of Old World traditions and advances in technology, to use wood creatively in the home.

This book attempts to place the wooden house into a historical and social context, revealing its various structural skeletons and different styles of interiors through the centuries, tracing the development of wood as an integral design element in international architectural history, and providing inspiration for anyone who appreciates a natural way of life.

Judith Miller

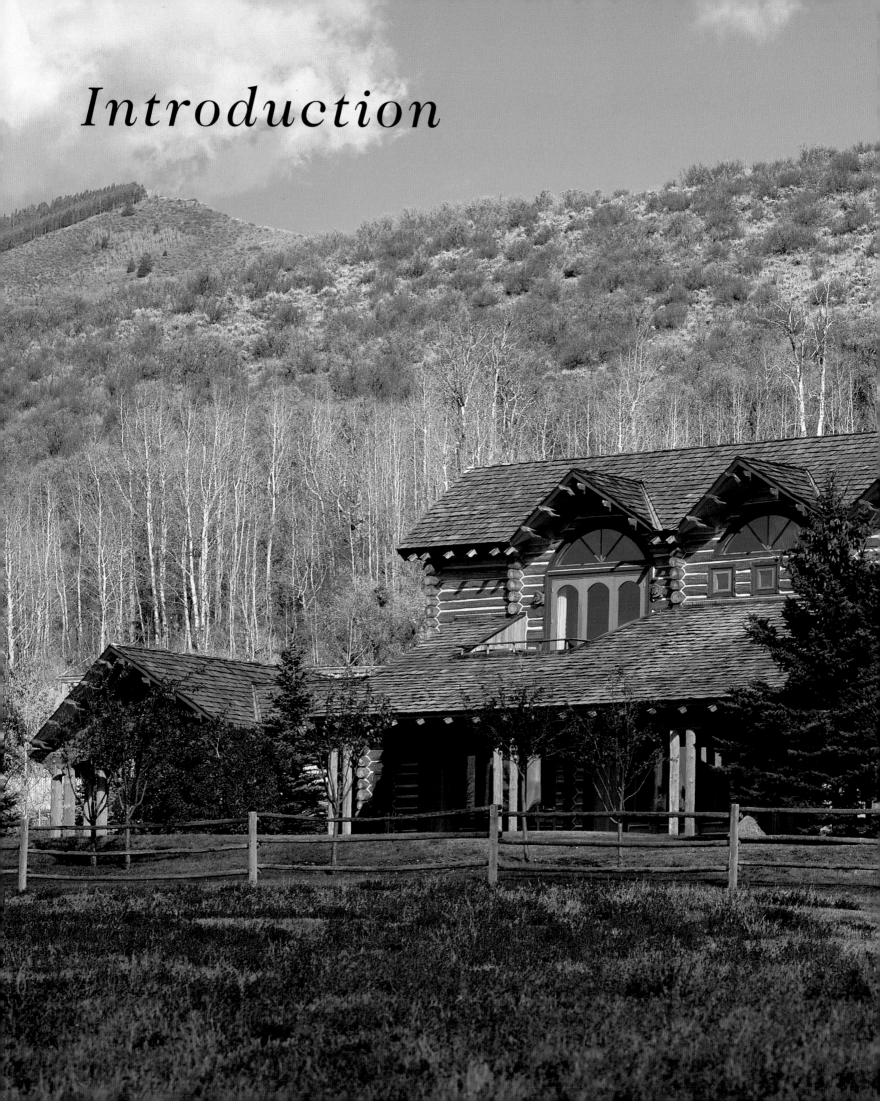

Introduction

Building with Wood

Throughout the world, timber has played a fundamental role in the history of mankind and the growth of civilization. From the beginning of time, wood has been used to make fires to provide warmth, light and cooking facilities, and it has served as a highly versatile raw material for making a wide range of tools and domestic artefacts, for crafting furniture, and for building ships and houses. Over the centuries, wood's structural properties and unique aesthetic qualities have ensured its continued use in all these areas, with an ever-increasing wealth of new techniques, designs and finishes to be explored.

From the Middle Ages until the Industrial Revolution in the 18th and 19th centuries, when steam power was harnessed allowing timber to be sawn by machine, and mass-production techniques were introduced for efficiently producing tools and building components, most of the population of Europe and Scandinavia was heavily reliant on locally available timber to construct shelter and accommodation. Before the 18th century, bricks were made in relatively small quantities and, due to their weight, they were difficult to transport over great distances until the establishment of the railway network. Building houses with bricks was thus largely the preserve of the wealthiest sections of society. Similarly, apart from in areas where suitable stone was close at hand, the high cost of quarrying and transporting stone rendered it a building material largely confined to civic and religious architecture, and large baronial and aristocratic houses. Wood, however, remained in plentiful supply throughout much of Europe, and houses constructed either wholly or partly from wood proliferated in both rural and urban areas.

In rural regions with dense forestation, such as large parts of Sweden and Norway, the Swiss and Austrian Alps, and central and eastern Germany, many wooden houses were built with logs, their walls consisting of round or flat-sided logs secured horizontally on top of one another and usually notched together at the corners. Given the extremely cold winters suffered in these areas, one of the main advantages of building in this manner was the considerable degree of insulation provided by the large mass of the log walls. However, in urban areas, and in rural regions where the forests were less extensive, log construction simply was not a viable proposition – transporting the quantity of timber required to build a log house was either impossible, too time-consuming, or too expensive. Consequently, a method of building with wood that made more economical use of the raw material was devised.

The timber-framed houses built in Europe and Scandinavia before the Industrial Revolution incorporated, on average, two-fifths of the quantity of wood needed to make a log house of equivalent size. Although different methods of timber framing were employed, notably cruck framing and box framing, the basic principles of construction remained the same: the walls were built from a series of interlocking vertical and horizontal sawn timbers, which were reinforced in places with diagonal or curved braces and combined with roof trusses, purlins and rafters to make the skeletal framework of the building (see Glossary, p. 186, for a definition of these and other terms). Except where windows and doors were inserted, the spaces in the wall frame were filled with non-structural panels of either wattle and daub, or lath and plaster or, occasionally, bricks (also known as nogging); roofs were of thatch, tiles or, less often, wooden boards. The majority of early European timber-framed houses, in which the vertical posts and studs, and the horizontal sills and cross-rails were left exposed, were colloquially referred to as half-timbered. However, at a later date, many of these houses were covered with horizontal wooden boards (known as weatherboards, or clapboards) to

protect the infill panels from the elements and provide a greater degree of insulation – a practice that began in Scandinavia, where weatherboards were often applied at the time of construction.

Although many Native Americans had a long tradition of building with wood, a vast repertoire of skills necessary for the construction of log and timber-framed houses crossed the Atlantic with the European and Scandinavian carpenters who emigrated to the new colonies of North America during the 17th and 18th centuries. Such skills were not only in great demand by the rapidly expanding population, but were also well suited to a continent with vast quantities of wood yet to be exploited. Log and timber-framed houses proliferated in the USA, just as they had earlier in Europe and Scandinavia. Moreover, considerable impetus was given to the construction of weatherboard timber-framed houses in the early 19th century, when a revolutionary method of construction was devised in Chicago. Exploiting the invention of cheap, mass-produced nails (which had previously been made individually by hand), and more uniform timber from the mechanized sawmills, balloon framing dispensed with the skilled, labour-intensive job of securing the vertical and horizontal members of the frame with mortise-and-tenon joints, and simply involved nailing the horizontal timbers to the vertical studs. As a result, it became easier, quicker and cheaper to build wooden houses. The greater flexibility of the technique also made it possible for architects and builders to construct these houses in a wide variety of contemporary and period-revival styles – developments that did much to make timber-frame construction widespread in Australia and New Zealand when they were colonized by European immigrants during the 19th century.

In many respects, the Industrial Revolution was something of a double-edged sword as far as the construction of wooden houses was concerned. In Europe, it coincided with the dwindling of timber resources, and the combination resulted in brick construction replacing timber framing as the primary method of building residential houses – although the manufacture and installation of wooden architectural fixtures and fittings, such as doors, windows, floors, staircases and panelling, continued unabated and

actually benefited from the mechanization of the timber industry. In most of Scandinavia and many parts of the USA, where timber remained in reasonably plentiful supply, the construction of balloon-framed and log houses was sustained by the new efficiencies of the timber industry – to the extent that the majority of residential homes built in the USA today are made of wood.

Choosing to live in a log or timber-framed house is a symbol of the revival and celebration of a pre-industrial, pre-technological age.

The new technologies of the 19th and 20th centuries have resulted in other, supposedly more durable, building materials usurping the pre-eminence of timber. Chief among these is concrete, which is cheaper than wood and brick, and more versatile than the latter since it can be moulded into any shape; when reinforced with metal rods, it is also extremely strong. However, initial optimism as to its durability has been undermined by the discovery that it can be prone to disintegration (concrete cancer) in a relatively short time. Moreover, with the exception of committed Modernists, appreciation of its visual qualities in a residential context has rarely been greater than, at best, lukewarm.

It is, perhaps, no coincidence that the alienation many have come to feel in relation to concrete-built accommodation during the second half of the 20th century has been accompanied by a widespread re-appreciation of the constructional and aesthetic qualities of wood, and of traditional timber-framed and log houses. The result has been a boom in wooden-house construction since the early 1970s – one that has been driven by post-Modernist architects and fuelled by consumer demand. To contemporary architects, the primary attraction of building with wood lies in the opportunity to explore the versatility of an organic rather than a man-made or synthetic material. To the home owner, the attraction of living in a log or timber-framed house runs deeper than that: it symbolizes a revival and a celebration of a pre-industrial, pre-technological age, in which traditional methods and standards of craftsmanship worked in harmony with, rather than exploited and rode roughshod over, Nature.

Architectural Styles

At the mention of wooden houses, different individuals will imagine completely different architectural styles, depending on where they live and the type of houses in which they grew up, and the extent of their travel experiences. To many, the wooden house is a rustic log cabin in the wilderness, a farmhouse designed in a manner true to the traditional Scandinavian style, or a Swiss mountain-side chalet; to others it is a suburban weatherboard house – whether in the small seaboard towns of New England, USA, or in cosmopolitan Auckland, New Zealand. The enormous variety of architectural styles employed in the construction of wooden houses is revealed – from the magnificent hewn-log farmhouse nestling in a

Work of Stephen Mack

Scandinavian valley, to the early Tudor half-timbered house in the English countryside, with its wonderfully

eccentric ceiling beams and floorboards, to the formal lines of an early Neoclassical mansion in the New

World colonies, with its covered, wide wooden veranda. What each style has in common is the use of wood as

a basic frame, and as the major building material for floors, walls and ceilings. The types of timber differ from

country to country and area to area, but the quality of the material speaks for itself in every location. That

natural timber, cut down from the living, breathing forest, should be manifested in myriad architectural

styles is a tribute to the imagination and practical skill of the architects and builders of each period.

Log Cabins and Lodges

'The form of architectural construction known as the log house, consisting of logs laid in a rectangle, one upon another, horizontally, and notched at the corners, is a very ancient form of European dwelling.' So wrote the Roman architect Vitruvius early in the 1st century BC, and although the practice of building with logs is a primitive one, it has survived in forested regions around the world for the past 2,000 years, despite the development of more refined and less expensive wood-building techniques. The widespread appeal of the log house and all the romantic associations that it conjures up cannot be denied. It is this that has ensured the revival and reinterpretation of various methods and styles of log construction, particularly in the USA, where the idealistic view of the log house and the way of life it embraces are very much ingrained in the nation's psyche and are an important part of the cultural history.

Left This log house in Aspen, Colorado, USA, was inspired by Christian basilicas, Japanese Shinto shrines and the Great Camps of the Adirondack Mountains in New York. Surrounded by aspen and pine trees, the house, with its combination of huge, rough-hewn, 400-year-old larch logs and more refined sawn cedar facing, evokes a log temple.

Right Early 18th-century log farm buildings in Telemark, Norway.

Log buildings originated in the extensively forested regions of northern Europe and Scandinavia, and also in Russia. Until the latter part of the 19th century, this method of construction was fuelled by practical rather than aesthetic considerations. When hunting could no longer support an expanding population, forests were cleared to make way for livestock and arable farming, and the most efficient use for the felled trees was as building material for accommodation and storage. Even though log houses required more than twice as much wood as equivalent-sized timber-framed

Right An 18th-century farm moved from the village of Chatel to near Megève, France. The buildings of squared-log construction have been restored by master craftsmen using old timber and traditional techniques.

Left and above Details showing the construction of the walls of two log lofts in Telemark which date from the medieval period. The pine-log walls were built using the traditional Swedish coping method, where the underside of each log is hand-hewn to fit snugly onto the profile of the one below. Traditionally moss, earth, or pieces of cloth were used to caulk the gaps between the logs. The oval log ends are flush with the line of the wall – a profile described as 'plumb'.

houses, before the widespread introduction of mechanized saw-mills after the late 18th century, the easiest and quickest way to build was with roughly hewn logs laid horizontally on top of one another, rather than with planed and jointed wooden frames and planks, which were far more labour-intensive to produce by hand.

Log houses were favoured in areas of extreme temperatures since, provided they are accurately notched at the corners and

Left and right Two restored 18th-century farms from Savoy, France, built in the traditional way with squared, planed logs – a technique that has changed little since the Middle Ages.

Below A medieval loft in Telemark, constructed of squared pine logs on a stone base before the Black Death of 1350. These lofts were the first two-storey buildings on Norwegian farms and roughly 130 have survived, with about 70 in this valley alone. Their durability is possibly due to the large overhangs, which protect the wood at the base from rotting.

properly sealed along the joints, heavy log walls produce interiors that are warmer in winter and cooler in summer than timber-framed walls; the more mass incorporated into the structure, the less pronounced the temperature swings within it will be. As the temperature drops at night, the inside of the house retains its warmth as the logs gradually release the heat stored within their

Left and right Two chalets in Megève constructed in the traditional style from new squared and planed logs. The overhanging roofs, supported on simple wood brackets, help to protect the timber walls from rotting. The windows each have sturdy external wooden shutters that help to insulate the interiors against the severe winter cold.

In cold regions of Europe and Scandinavia, heavy log walls helped provide insulation against the freezing winter temperatures.

mass during the day. When the external temperature rises, the log walls take a while to warm up again and keep the inside cooler. In these regions, windows in log houses were small and oriented to the warmer south, often with external shutters. The steep pitched roofs had large overhangs to prevent heavy accumulations of snow, and many were insulated with sheets of birch bark covered with split wooden poles or turf. Large stone fireplaces were stoked during the day for cooking and heating, their long flues radiating warmth throughout the night. In summer, shutters and windows were opened, and sometimes the moss or turf used to caulk the gaps between the logs was removed to increase ventilation.

Softwoods, such as birch, cedar, spruce, fir and pine, have always been favoured over hardwoods for log construction due to their rapid growth cycle and the fact that they are easy to cut, shape and stain. Logs can either be stripped of their bark and cambium (the outer layer of sapwood) or left with them intact. This was often the choice on the American frontier where speedy construction was necessary and manpower was in short supply, but these logs were more vulnerable to decay as a result of moisture retention. The majority of logs now leave sawmills peeled and fairly uniform in diameter; bark-on logs are more unusual and are

specifically chosen to enhance the rustic appearance of a house. A compromise can be achieved by skip peeling, a process that removes virtually all of the bark, but leaves some of the cambium intact, resulting in a natural-looking mottled surface.

Another key element in determining the look of a log house is the profile of the logs making up the walls. Among the most common are fully round; flat on the sides with the top and bottom left round; flat on the top and bottom with the sides left round; round top and sides, but scribed, or 'saddle notched', along the bottom to fit onto the top of the log below; and flat on the top, bottom and inner side with a round outer side. Although there are many exceptions, fully round and round-sided logs are common in the USA, except in the east where flat-sided logs – prevalent in Europe

Below A farm-workers' log lodge built near Elverum in c. 1830. Elverum market was a centre for commerce, and the foreign influence introduced by the international trade probably accounts for the area's painted exteriors.

and Scandinavia – are favoured. The ends of the logs, where they are notched together at the corners of a house, also contribute significantly to its appearance. There is a wide variety of profiles and among the most popular are the 'beaver cut', where the log ends are cut like roughly sharpened pencils; the 'butt and run', where the ends are squared off to create notches that resemble dovetail joints; the 'plumb end', where the ends of the fully round logs extend a little way beyond the face of the wall; and the 'diamond notch', in which the ends are shaped like four-pointed diamonds.

Two traditional methods of making log walls are scribing and chinking. Scribing, or Swedish coping, originated in Scandinavia and is the older method. It involves cutting a shallow U-shaped groove, or saddle notch, along the bottom of a log to match the profile of the top of the log beneath it, so each log sits tightly on top of another. The unseasoned logs shrink as they dry out, making the walls relatively weatherproof. Hand-scribing was a time-consuming and skilled craft, and in dry areas excessive shrinkage opened up the joints which then required caulking. It was rarely used in the USA before the 1970s, when new methods for peeling

and scribing logs by machine made it more viable. Chinking involves laying a mortar-like mix between the logs to bond them; prior to the 19th century, this consisted of hay or pine twigs, and clay, and later a form of cement. Chinking allowed rapid construction and could compensate for irregularly shaped logs, but as the wood dried out the logs shrank away from the mix and created gaps. Modern architects take into account and compensate for the fact that even fully seasoned logs shrink to a degree. Also, the development of new acrylic latex chinking compounds, which cure but do not harden, and flexible caulking compounds that can be used to fill cracks and gaps, have helped to solve the problem.

Two of the most common log-house roofs are 'raftered', where the roof is made up of log rafters laid perpendicular to the ridge log (which forms the apex of the roof), and 'purlin', where the roof is made up of logs running parallel to the ridge and supported at intervals by vertical posts. Raftered roofs were originally favoured because the rafters, which were shorter and thinner than purlins, were easier to lift into place. However, differential settling between the ridge log and the plate logs on top of the walls often resulted in structural problems – notably the displacement of the walls. In modern constructions this is overcome either by using collar ties to hold the rafters in place, or by spanning the walls

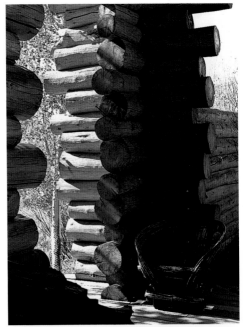

This page and opposite Architect Jim Ruscitto designed this house in Sun Valley, Idaho, USA, with a combination of logs, stucco, rock and glass to create an efficient passive solar system. Built among native willows and tall grasses, the house is constructed of logs and taupe-coloured stucco that blend into the environment. The earth-coloured walls are built over a small stream, on pilings concealed by rocks. The log ends protrude into the surrounding decks, creating a series of private courtyards. A criss-cross pattern is formed by the geometric cubicles of adobe pueblos, which contrast with the logs' linear forms.

many modern structures where vast distances are spanned, the framework and joints are usually reinforced with steel pins.

Although contemporary log houses are often ground-breaking in design, the influence of traditional log buildings, such as the basic cabin of the early American pioneer, cannot be denied. The widely held belief that log construction was first brought to North America in the 17th century by the European settlers is not strictly true, since Native Americans living in forested regions had been building log dwellings and fortifications for centuries before the colonies were established. However, there is no doubt that many tribes were influenced by the influx of European styles and methods of building, and by the mid-1820s many had abandoned their traditional earthen huts for dwellings constructed of hewn logs.

When the settlers arrived, about 40 per cent of the land was forested, and this, together with the harsh climate, made log buildings the obvious choice – especially for immigrants with expertise in log construction. As the growing population spread across the continent, thousands of log dwellings were built to

with floor joists. Purlin roofs are favoured now that modern machinery is available to lift the heavy logs, and because they are better able to tolerate settling than raftered roofs.

In modern log houses, architects often make a feature of the interior support posts by using character logs, or they reduce the number needed with the use of trusses to allow more scope for the layout of the interior. The revival of post-and-beam construction has also allowed architects more freedom. With this method, walls are either constructed of vertical posts infilled with fully round or flat-sided logs, or a structural frame of log posts, girders and roof beams is made, which can be filled in with another material. In

provide accommodation. Broadly, they can be divided into two types: the first pioneers' simple huts and cabins, and the later settlers' more sophisticated hewn-log ranches, lodges and barns. Many basic cabins were hastily built by the pioneers during the rush for land and fortune on the rapidly extending frontiers. Crudely assembled from round, unseasoned, ill-fitting logs with the bark and sapwood often left intact, they were vulnerable to the elements, and few survived for more than a generation or two. As settlements became established, areas of forest were cleared for ranching, farming and mining, and houses were built for a more permanent existence, generally with de-barked, seasoned logs, each of which was carefully hand-scribed and profiled to fit snugly onto the one below. Unlike the early cabins, most of these structures were relatively weatherproof and less prone to decay.

Many immigrants to Australia and New Zealand during the 19th century also found that areas of densely wooded land, and the need for cheap accommodation that was quick to build provided the impetus for log construction. Yet for centuries the Maori people had been building ponga houses, in which tree trunks were laid horizontally within a timber frame.

For practical reasons, the building of log houses should have entered a terminal decline when mechanized sawmills became widespread and allowed the components for wooden frames to be produced quickly, cheaply and in vast quantities. Where brick or stone were unavailable or too expensive, the inhabitants of forested regions increasingly favoured timber-frame construction. Many log structures were taken apart and their hewn logs milled to make the components for larger, lighter timber-framed buildings. However, despite the cost-effectiveness of timber framing and its flexibility in terms of style and design, log houses enjoyed a revival in the USA at the end of the 19th century, fuelled primarily by romance and aesthetics rather than practicality.

The revival began with the building of the Great Camps in the Adirondack Mountains in New York State during the late 1880s. The camps comprised a series of massive log lodges designed by architects under the leadership of William West Durant as fashionable rustic retreats for wealthy families such as the Vanderbilts and the Carnegies. They drew inspiration from many sources, in particular the cabins of early pioneers like Davy Crockett and

Daniel Boone, the 18th- and 19th-century lumber and mining camps of the Adirondacks, and Alpine chalets. Featuring unpeeled logs, with bark, branch and twig decoration, the camps inspired similar retreats across the country. Despite the fact that these lodges were, unlike the frontier houses on which they were modelled, architect-designed, expensive playthings of the rich, their significance lay in their affinity with the frontier spirit and the desire to return to a simple, self-sufficient, honest lifestyle. The

This page and opposite This lodge
nestles at the base of the Rocky
Mountains, near Aspen, Colorado.
It was inspired by the log cabins in
the Great Camps of the Adirondacks. The house was constructed
with untreated pine logs that were
felled in Yellowstone National Park
from standing-dead trees which
had been scorched by a catastrophic fire. Standing-dead trees,
which have normally been killed
either by fire or beetle, are usually
left upright for several years before
being felled. Well-seasoned, sturdy
and environmentally friendly, they
are often used for log construction
in the USA. The lodge is built on a
base of massive boulders, and the
coped logs have an infill of polymer
chinking that allows for the wood's
natural shrinkage. Overlooking
the North Star Nature Preserve
and surrounded by aspen trees,
the lodge blends into its environment, reflecting the design
principle of the Great Camps.

Above The massive logs that
make up the structure
dominate the exterior, which
is divided up by the series of
wooden decks.

Left The lodge is reached by
a wide split-log stairway,
with a stair rail and
balusters of large branches.

promotion of the log house as a source of moral rectitude and
civic pride was further fuelled by the Roosevelt Administration
during the Great Depression of the 1930s. As part of a government
plan to reduce unemployment, thousands of out-of-work labour-
ers were recruited to build a series of traditional log lodges, ranger
stations, lookout towers and bridges in America's national parks.

During the 1960s and 1970s, the back-to-nature movement
that had manifested itself in the USA in the late 19th century

re-emerged, and the log house was discovered by a new generation wishing to drop out of the rat race of modern commercial and industrial life. Underpinning this movement was a philosophy that advocated communal self-sufficiency and equated spiritual well-being with a return to the land. Energy-efficient log houses were the ideal choice of accommodation, since unlike concrete, glass and steel, wood does not disturb the earth's magnetic field and can breathe, helping to naturally ventilate interiors and purify the air. Above all, logs had unique decorative and textural qualities that provided a physical and emotional link with nature unmatched by most forms of modern architecture. The appeal spread to the general population and in the 1980s many specialist companies were established to meet the growing demand for pre-cut log-house kits, most of which were built as holiday homes for middle- and upper-income families. By the 1990s nearly all log houses were being built as primary residences, and thousands of kits are exported around the world – even to regions with no tradition of log construction. This can partly be attributed to the emotional and romantic appeal of the log house, but has also been fuelled by the increasing involvement of architects and specialist builders who have brought many aspects of log-house construction to the cutting edge of design and engineering technology.

The definition of 'Rustic work' in a late 19th-century dictionary:
'Where woodwork is used it is customary to provide a continuous sheathing as of boards upon which is nailed the small logs and branches with their bark, moss, etc, carefully preserved.'

Left and above The wooden veranda is furnished with Adirondacks-style furniture made by a local craftsman, Dave Fritchley, from branches collected for their interesting shapes from the surrounding woods. Although the furniture takes inspiration from that of the Adirondacks, the locally gathered materials, fashioned by the hands of an English craftsman, lend it a more native feel. Local branches are also used for the balustrade, which helps to blend the cabin into the mature wooded landscape.

Far left and below The Gothic-style arched door and window frames feature meticulous, detailed rustic decoration, with elaborate patterns made up of twig work and pine cones.

Opposite The rustic guest cottage in the grounds of a manor house in Sussex, England, takes inspiration from the Great Camps of the Adirondacks in New York State. The cabin was constructed with a framework of six squared telegraph poles and the walls are faced with split logs.

Half-timbered Houses

Quintessentially British, the traditional half-timbered house, made up of an interlocking wooden frame filled in with wattle and daub, can still be found in many villages in northern Europe. Its influence can also be seen throughout the world in the wide range of building styles it inspired.

Other than in areas rich in stone, most dwellings were built of cob or wood until the late 18th century, with bricks – expensive and not widely available – mainly used only for grand houses, fireplaces and chimneys. Clearing forests for farming provided the ideal raw material, and timber framing became the most popular form of building in many regions where log construction was inappropriate. Depending on climate, fashion, and the quality of the wood, the framework and infill material were either clad – with planks, lime render, stucco or brick – or left exposed in a style known as half-timbering. The harsh climates in Scandinavia, North America, Australia and New Zealand encouraged builders to sheath timber-framed houses with boards to protect them from the elements and improve insulation. Whereas the milder climate and less plentiful supply of wood in much of northern Europe contributed to the custom of leaving timber-framed walls exposed.

Left Abernodwydd Farmhouse, built in Powys, Wales, in 1678, now at Cardiff's Museum of Welsh Life, is typical of the area. Its frame, infilled with wattle and daub, is set on a stone sill to prevent the wood rotting; its roof is straw with a hazel underthatch.

In northern Europe two methods of constructing timber-framed buildings were developed: cruck framing and box framing. In both, large wall frames of vertical and horizontal timbers, usually oak, were combined with roof trusses, purlins and rafters to create the skeleton. This was invariably preassembled off the site where adjustments could easily be made, and all the components were numbered before it was dismantled for transportation to the site.

Box-framed buildings were made up of a series of square or rectangular timber-framed boxes, known as bays. The end walls of each, the gable panels, had roof gable structures attached to distribute the weight of the roof down through the corner posts. Originally, a frame's vertical members were driven directly into the ground, but from the Middle Ages it was usual to build a low stone wall on which heavy timber beams were placed; the bays were then erected on top of these sills. All but the poorest houses consisted of more than one roofed bay, with long timber purlins joining the roof trusses of each. Lengths of sawn timber could easily be joined to increase the size of each wall panel, and more bays could be added. A relatively large open space for a main hall, the

focus of medieval life, could be created by leaving out the lower sections of cross framing at the gable ends of two adjoining bays. However, this could not be done extensively as to do so would weaken the structural framework.

Crucks were large, slightly curved timbers, generally made by sawing in half a large, curved tree trunk. They were erected in

Above Built as a parsonage after 1516, Headcorn Manor in Kent, England, is a restored medieval Wealden house – a type of timber-framed house peculiar to the Weald in southeast England and characterized by a central open hall flanked by bays of two storeys.

Left Now at the Museum of Welsh Life, Hendre'r-Ywydd Uchaf Farmhouse was built in the Vale of Clwyd, Wales, in c. 1508 and was the home of a well-to-do farmer. Its name means 'old settlement of the yew trees'. Built on stone foundations, the house is timber-framed with the thatch roof supported by five crucks. The wattle infill panels are made from hazel rods woven around split oak uprights. Both the panels and frame have been coated with white limewash for protection.

Left *Nant Wallter Cottage was built in Dyfed, Wales, between 1760 and 1780, and has been re-located in Cardiff as part of the Museum of Welsh Life. The cottage is an example of a traditional cruck-framed structure, and has two pairs of jointed crucks that support the straw thatch roof, which is laid on a base of woven hazel wattle. The white lime-washed walls are made of 'clom' (a mixture of clay, stones and straw or bracken).*

Above *Smallhythe Place, near Tenterden in Kent – now the home of the Ellen Terry Museum – was built after a great fire in 1516. The upper storey overhangs the lower storey all the way across the front of the house, increasing the stability of the structure and creating more spacious rooms upstairs. The close-studded oak framework is left untreated with the infill painted buff; the quantity of timber used suggests the affluence of the original owner.*

pairs that were joined at the top with a collar or tie beam to form an A-shape. The crucks extended from the ground to the ridge of the roof and served the same structural function as the gable panels in box-framed buildings. The curved upper sections formed the profile of the roof and bore the roof purlins and rafters, and the straighter lower parts acted as the corner posts for the timber-framed walls, transmitting the weight of the roof directly to the ground without the need for a separate gable structure. Another advantage was that whereas box-framed buildings were divided by the gable panels between each bay, it was possible to incorporate much longer, uninterrupted spaces within a cruck-framed structure. The drawback was that the size of a building was dependent on the timber available, since several trees of roughly equal height and profile were required to build a house of more than one bay.

Right and far right Hartnup House in Smarden, Kent, sits below St Michael's church, which was built of stone in the 14th century. The house is dated 1671, but this relates to the gable and the bay window below it – the rest of the building is actually 16th century.

A technique known as aisle framing combined both methods in the same building to increase the overall width. On either side of each pair of crucks additional posts and framing were erected to form new outer walls, creating aisles along both sides of the main building over which the roof was usually extended in a continuous sweep. Although this created more floor space, it restricted the amount of light that could enter the main building, producing a fairly gloomy interior. Lack of light was already a

Above, left to right Chessenden
House is a large medieval half-
timbered house in Smarden and is
an excellent example of the typical
Wealden arrangement of an open
hall in between two-storey jettied
wings, with a simple hipped roof.
In the 17th century a second floor
was inserted into the hall and the
two-storey canted bay and gable
were added.

Right Dragon House in Smarden
is an L-shaped medieval structure,
with 17th-century alterations,
including the decorative frieze
depicting dragons.

problem in timber-framed houses, as invariably windows and doors were allotted the relatively narrow spaces between vertical studs in the framework, with the horizontal members left out and diagonal braces inserted to reinforce the wall. The occasional vertical stud could be left out to allow for a wider opening, but this was generally avoided so as not to weaken the structure.

An important development for the strength of the timber-framed house was the introduction of jettying during the early 14th century. The beams and joists of the lower storey were extended beyond one or more external wall and supported by brackets or corner posts. The overhanging upper storey was then built up on a wooden sill secured onto the beams and joists. The projection not only increased the size of the rooms on the upper storey, it also acted as a cantilever, producing a more stable structure. The popularity of jetties fell in the early 17th century when laws to conserve timber for ship building were enforced and governments, concerned about the risk of fires in narrow city streets, began to promote the use of non-flammable brick and stone.

The amount of timber used in the wall frames of a house depended on the quality and abundance of wood in the area, and

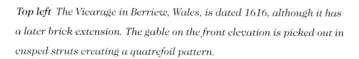

Top left *The Vicarage in Berriew, Wales, is dated 1616, although it has a later brick extension. The gable on the front elevation is picked out in cusped struts creating a quatrefoil pattern.*

Above *This early 18th-century house in Berriew is fairly retrospective in construction: the transverse braces are more commonly associated with half-timbered buildings of the late 17th century.*

Right and top right *Berrington Manor near Shrewsbury, England, is an early to mid-15th-century priest's hall house (the right-hand part) that was extended in 1658. The cusped struts are both decorative and structural.*

Opposite *Weobley, near Hereford, England, is rich in 14th- and 15th-century timber-framed buildings. This house, The Throne, c. 1600, is a retrospective structure that is simple in form for this date.*

on the affluence of the householder. Where timber was scarce poorer houses featured thin, widely spaced frames with large infill panels, but in areas rich in good-quality hardwoods, grander houses usually incorporated more timber, often thickly cut. Close studding, geometric patterns and cusped or curved braces within the panelling are all signs of prosperity, as are carved, pierced or moulded posts, wall plates, bargeboards, doors and window hoods.

The oldest and most widely used infill material was wattle and daub. Oak staves were secured within each section of the framework, vertically in open frames and horizontally in close-studded ones. Thin branches, usually of supple hazel, were woven through the staves and daubed on both sides with a mixture of sand, lime,

The look of a half-timbered house could be dramatically altered by the choice of finish for the wooden frame and the infill panels in between. Styles not only varied from region to region, but changed with the advent of new techniques and were subject to the whims of fashion.

Below Brookgate is one of the oldest manor houses on the Shropshire border between England and Wales. The earliest part was built in 1350 as a single-range (a structure extending in one direction) open to the roof – except for the inclusion of a sleeping loft at one end, now used as a sitting room. In 1500 a wing was added, making a classic L-shape. The far end of the earlier medieval structure was destroyed in 1612 and a new parlour was built, creating the traditional Elizabethan layout of a central hall flanked by two wings. The house has been completely restored by the architect and timber-frame specialist Graham Moss, who added the cast-iron brackets for the guttering on the side elevation (bottom left). The original Elizabethan manor would not have had guttering, but the simple Arts and Crafts style of these brackets blends well with the character of the earlier structure.

chopped straw and dung. The first coat was pressed into the gaps and the surface keyed for another layer which was worked smooth. Even in a mild climate it was necessary to apply several layers of white limewash, initially and every couple of years, to waterproof the panels and act as a mild fungicide and insecticide. In some regions flat laths of oak or chestnut were woven through the staves, producing a reasonably weatherproof panel that could be left undaubed. Until the late 18th century the use of bricks was rare, except where they were manufactured locally, but after the Industrial Revolution cheaper bricks became widely available, and many wattle-and-daub panels were replaced with this more durable material. Bricklaying patterns varied from region to region and simpler designs, such as English or Flemish bond, were used in lesser houses and more intricate diamond or herringbone patterns in grander buildings. Sometimes brickwork was plastered and whitewashed to imitate the original wattle and daub.

Although timber frames of high-quality oak were often left in their natural state, prior to the 19th century most framing was protected with limewash which gave the wood a silvery patina. Less commonly, the timber was treated with ox blood, creating a red-brown hue, and in wet regions a primitive water-based paint with a charcoal pigment was applied. In the 19th century a method was developed in England's West Midlands which involved painting the timbers with tar or pitch produced by distilling coal. This technique, known as black-and-white work, created a striking contrast between the frame and the limewashed infill. The look quickly became fashionable in northern Europe and hundreds of timber-framed houses were redecorated in this style.

Although by the early 19th century more durable methods of building with brick, stone and cement had replaced timber-frame construction in northern Europe, the timeless beauty of the traditional half-timbered house inspired a range of styles. In the USA, Stick-style houses of the 1860s and 1870s featured decorative stickwork, mostly on gable ends and upper storeys, symbolizing the structural skeleton of the building. Some American Queen Anne houses of 1880–1910 had half-timbered masonry, and many 20th-century Tudor-style cottages of the American Beaux-Arts movement incorporated features of half-timbering, such as porch roofs supported on square timbers with thick corner braces,

Top At Stokesay Castle in Shropshire, a Jacobean gatehouse stands at the entrance to a 13th-century fortified manor house. Quatrefoil patterning was typical of the Welsh Marches, but such elaborate decoration on a modest gatehouse would indicate the substantial wealth of the owner.

Above Pitchford Hall in Shropshire was totally restored in the 19th century. The house is a traditional box-frame construction – a flexible method of building that allowed extra rooms to be relatively easily added as required.

exposed beam ends with carved finials, and brackets with foliate or animal motifs. Many of British architect Sir Edwin Lutyens' Arts and Crafts houses were half-timbered, as were the early 20th-century mock-Tudor houses. But the architectural heritage of the half-timbered house is most evident in the 'Tudorbethan' houses of the 1920s and 1930s that dominate the English garden suburbs. These wood-adorned houses are modern testaments to the enduring appeal of the skilfully built medieval manor house.

Weatherboard Houses

The weatherboard, or clapboard, house is intrinsically linked to the New World. Its name conjures up images of early colonial timber-framed houses clad in cedar boards, weathered by the rain and sun, or painted in natural shades of white, cream, blue, yellow or green. It was the most practical form of architecture in countries with good supplies of timber, with cladding to provide insulation and protection from the elements. The layout was simple, with a front door into a central hallway from which rooms led off on either side. The nature of the facade allowed architects great stylistic versatility and a plethora of styles developed, from the ornately carved and decorated 'Painted Ladies' of the USA to Australia's sprawling 'Queenslanders' with their shady verandas.

Left and below Burr Tavern is a white-pine weatherboard house, built in c. 1835 in East Meredith on the mail route to New York City, USA. Originally coated with white lead paint, its owner, paint specialist Chris Ohrstrom, has repainted it in yellow ochre.

Right A weatherboard late Colonial-style house, in Greenwich Village, New York. The six-over-six sliding sash windows, each flanked by external louvred shutters, are arranged symmetrically across the front and side elevations in classical Georgian style. The simple, carved and moulded wooden door hood is also typical of the mid-18th century.

Far right This merchant's house on the edge of a fjord near Bergen, Norway, dates from c. 1690, with an extension built in the 1840s, when weatherboarding – also known locally as panelling – was applied. The front of the house, which faces the harbour, was painted white as a sign of status, while the back was coated in much cheaper red paint.

Right A Norwegian timber-framed barn, colourwashed in yellow ochre. The building dates from the Middle Ages, but the tiled roof is probably late 18th century.

By the 18th century, timber resources began to diminish in parts of northern Europe and brick and stone gradually replaced wood as the primary building material. Yet the abundant supply of timber in Scandinavia, North America, Australia and New Zealand has ensured that in many areas timber-frame construction is still favoured over building with brick or concrete.

The different characteristics of vernacular houses from region to region can largely be ascribed to builders responding to the climate and topography of the land and, particularly before the advent of mass production and the development of an extensive transport system, the availability of local materials. With the exception of Denmark – where many houses were built of stone or clay – the dense forestation in Scandinavia promoted both log and timber-frame construction on a wide scale. The countries' harsh winters and heavy snowfalls led to the majority of timber-framed houses being sheathed with overlapping horizontal or vertical

Top right and far right Militia House in Smarden, Kent, England, is a timber-framed structure which was weatherboarded in the late 18th century. The dentil cornice, consisting of a set of square or rectangular blocks evenly spaced to form an ornamental row, is typical of the area.

Right Unlike Militia House (above), The Battery, built to billet sailors training on the Kent coast, was weatherboarded at the time of construction in 1873. The majority of English weatherboard houses are painted white, but The Battery has always been blue because of its association with the navy.

Left and far left The Isaac Stevens House in Wethersfield, Connecticut, USA, was built in 1788–9 for a prominent leather worker. While the front of the house, which faces the main square, was quite elaborate to indicate the owner's status, the back (shown here) was much simpler. There are few communities in the USA as old as Wethersfield; with 200 houses built before 1850, it is the largest historic district in Connecticut.

boards, known as weatherboards, which protected the walls from the wind, rain and snow, and helped to insulate the interiors.

The practice of cladding timber-framed houses with wood has its roots in the Norwegian stave churches built during the 12th and 13th centuries. These consisted of a very strong skeletal framework of load-bearing wooden posts and beams, to the exterior of which vertical wooden staves were secured. Mainly due to the inherent strength of their post-and-beam construction, such buildings were highly resistant to the stresses of winter storms and heavy accumulations of snow. The custom of applying wood cladding to the exterior of a timber frame was widely adopted in

In 17th- and 18th-century America, most settlers – whether they came from Britain or central Europe – lived with one foot in the Old World.

Right and far right The Hempstead House in New London, Connecticut, dates from 1678 and, due to Joshua Hempstead's diary detailing all improvements and repairs, it is one of the best-documented vernacular houses of the 17th century. The main part of the house is oak, with a new wing built 50 years later, mainly of pine. Leaded lights were cheaper than wooden sashes and were quite common in this area until c. 1770; these original windows were imported from England.

Above and right The Buttolph Williams House was built in Wethersfield in c. 1715, although it was quite retrospective in style. The house was constructed on stone foundations with oak post-and-beam structural members and wooden shingles.

Scandinavia during the middle of the 17th century when mechanized sawmills, which appeared earlier there than in the rest of Europe, began to produce cheaply and easily the uniform timber required for framing and cladding. By the early 19th century, ornamental Dragon- or Viking-style architecture began to appear in Sweden and subsequently spread to Denmark and Norway. A combination of log and timber-frame construction, Dragon-style villas, hotels, sanatoriums and railway stations incorporated horizontal and vertical timber cladding, together with a wealth of decorative details including ornate brackets and balustrades, with motifs such as dragon figureheads and other seafaring symbols as an expression of pride in the Viking Age. Although the Swedes and Danes tired of Dragon style during the 1880s, the Norwegians continued to build in this style throughout the late 19th century as a symbol of their struggle to dissolve their union with Sweden.

During the 18th and 19th centuries, many half-timbered houses in Britain and the non-mountainous regions of northern Europe were also weatherboarded – usually horizontally – for ease of maintenance, rather than having their wattle-and-daub infill panels repaired or replaced. However, once bricks became less

costly and more widely available as a result of the Industrial Revolution, many half-timbered houses were encased with brick.

European settlers first established roots on the eastern seaboard of North America at the beginning of the 17th century and they gradually extended their cultures across the continent, introducing their traditional methods of timber-frame construction which flourished in the densely forested land. All but the grandest of Colonial buildings were made of wood, with bricks and stone generally reserved for chimneys and foundations – even when houses were built of brick or stone, their roofs, fences, porches, window and door frames were usually made of wood. Half-timbered houses were built by German settlers in North Carolina and Wisconsin, and by the French in the Mississippi Valley and on the Gulf Coast – in the case of the latter, these usually took the form of vertical timber posts infilled with rendered earth or stone. However, the severity of the climate in many areas soon resulted in most settlers adapting their traditional methods of building by cladding the timber-framed walls with sawn or split weatherboards and replacing thatched roofs with wooden shingles.

A variety of regional styles developed during the Colonial period. For example, many houses in the southern colonies had a main ground floor and a single-space loft, steeply pitched gables, often with dormers, and brick chimneys at one or both ends. In

Above A small 19th-century weatherboard cottage in Massachusetts, USA.

Right and above right Chase Hill Farm in Rhode Island, USA, is a one-storey 'Cape Cod' house built in 1792 and restored by Stephen Mack. The typical Cape Cod house, with a central chimney, was the most common house type in New England. The oak trees that make its post-and-beam frame were squared by hewers, then marked up and mortised and tenoned by housewrights. The weatherboards were hand-split and shaved to a fairly uniform width.

Below and bottom The Joseph Webb House in Wethersfield was constructed in the late 18th century and is a fine example of the houses built for the affluent Connecticut 'River God' families, who made their fortunes by trading via the Connecticut River. The design of the building – both outside and inside – is in keeping with the Classical style of architecture that was fashionable in North America during this period.

Above Located at Chase Hill Farm, this one-room 'stone-ender', with an Elizabethan-style stone pilaster chimney stack, was built in Rhode Island by English settlers in the 17th century. Stone-enders, which have one gable end built of stone, are unique to Rhode Island.

New England, many of the larger houses built during the latter part of the 17th century featured English Tudor and Elizabethan elements, such as a jettied second storey, a massive central chimney, few windows and low ceilings. To many of these buildings rear extensions with steeply sloping roofs, known as lean-tos or saltboxes, were added at a later date.

During the Federal era, the 60 or so years that followed the end of the American Colonial period up until the early 1840s, a tremendous number of timber-framed houses were built, with many stylistic elements borrowed from English Adam style. Improved techniques for cutting and shaping wood, together with the invention of machine-cut nails, resulted in improvements in the quality of construction and a greater application of decorative detailing. The vast majority of timber-framed houses erected during this period were well made and clad with overlapping weatherboards, usually of pine and often beaded along the edges. Wooden single-entry porches became a popular addition in New England, while porticoes and double-tier verandas were fashionable in the Midwest and many southern states. Houses built in the Greek

Left, below left and below far left The Simon Huntington Tavern in Norwich, Connecticut, was built in 1703 and completely renovated in 1768. The structure is oak post and beam with hand-split laths fastened with hand-wrought nails. Oak, the choice of most English immigrant builders, was also the most abundant wood in this area. The exterior colour was accurately matched to samples of the original paint during a recent restoration by Stephen Mack.

to meet the urgent housing demands of the rapidly expanding population. A partial solution lay in the traditional practice of constructing timber frames in the carpenter's yard, where alterations could easily be made before the pieces were transported to the site and reassembled. This meant that numerous prefabricated timber-framed houses could be shipped across the Atlantic from northern Europe to the settlers on North America's east coast. However, while it was feasible to ship the heavy components for timber framing to new towns and cities on or close to the sea, transporting them overland was another matter, since the rail and road systems were not yet up to the task.

Right and far right This 1840s weatherboard house is adjoined to an 18th-century barn of traditional English construction moved from Stockbridge to Harvard, Massachusetts, and restored by Stephen Mack.

Revival and Neoclassical styles featured straight, square-cut, or vase-shaped wooden balustrades on verandas, walls and roofs.

While the quality of timber-framed houses and the sophistication of decorative detailing had advanced in leaps and bounds, the method of construction did have drawbacks. The building of a traditional cruck- or box-framed wooden house was a relatively slow process that demanded considerable skill. Sawing timber by hand, cutting mortise-and-tenon joints, routing grooves, drilling holes, shaping pegs and accurately assembling the structure required the specialist tools and training of highly skilled carpenters. Although the European colonists included many talented craftsmen in their number, there were simply not enough of them

An ingenious new method of timber-frame construction, known as balloon framing, was invented in Chicago in 1833. In combination with various technical advances – especially the mechanization of nail production and the development of steam-powered sawmills – this provided an extraordinarily efficient solution. Within two decades it had become the predominant means of building houses in the American urban west. Also known as basket framing, balloon framing gained its name because many traditional builders and carpenters, sceptical of the new method, thought the frame so light that it would blow away in the first strong wind. In fact, the balloon-framed house proved to be remarkably durable and made possible the fast-growing, high-

standard city and suburban American housing developments of the late 19th and early 20th centuries. Today, approximately three-quarters of the houses built in the USA are balloon-framed.

Probably the first balloon-framed building was St Mary's church in Chicago. Built by Augustine Taylor, a carpenter from Hartford, Connecticut, it consisted of a single storey, 11 metres long by 7.5 metres wide, covered by a low-pitched gable roof. The church was built in approximately three months and cost in the region of $400 – about half the time and money required to construct a similar-sized church using conventional timber-framing techniques. Soon after it was built, balloon-framed houses began to appear in Chicago at an amazing rate. In October 1834 a writer observed that while there had been only 50 balloon-framed houses in the city a year before, 'I counted them last Sunday and there was 628, and there is from one to four or five a day, and about 212 of them stores and groceries.' Records show that the average time from commission to completion was only one week.

The method of construction was simple. Instead of the thick posts and beams joined by pegged mortise-and-tenon joints that were used to create the heavy framework of traditional timber-framed houses, this technique employed a very light frame. The studs, wall plates, floor joists and roof rafters were of uniform, thin sawn timbers, butt jointed and nailed together so as to distribute the load or strain against the grain of the wood. The vertical studs ran from the sill to the eaves and the horizontal members were

Below An 1885 Queen Anne 'Painted Lady' in Aspen, Colorado, USA, painted in lilac, blue, red, green and saffron. 'Painted Lady' describes a facade decorated in at least three colours.

Below right A 'Painted Lady', built in Aspen in 1883 and decorated in the Mountain Stick style. The pattern on the brilliantly coloured gable is depicted with 25 colours, a Colorado trademark.

Bottom Roseland Cottage, 'The Pink House', was built in 1846 in Woodstock, Connecticut. With its perpendicular lines, the house is a wonderful example of high Gothic Revival architecture.

Opposite, left, below left to right, and bottom left The covered wooden veranda is an integral part of the weatherboard timber-framed houses prevalent throughout Australia and New Zealand. It was widely adopted by architects and builders in response to the extremities of the subtropical climate because it helped to ventilate and cool the walls and interior of the house while providing a shaded area for sitting, eating and even sleeping outside. To maximize airflow, most verandas incorporated lattice screens and fretwork balustrades – their degree of ornamentation primarily depending on the value of the house.

Far right The corner of this 19th-century house in Auckland, New Zealand, displays a range of architectural elements commonly associated with the Italianate style, fashionable in urban areas during the second half of the 19th century. Among these are the relatively broad eaves supported by brackets, and windows with tall, narrow proportions. The use of contrasting coloured paint on the weatherboard walls and on the window frames and surrounding architraves serves to accentuate the proportions of the various components.

nailed onto them. To the inside and outside of this basket-like cage any facing material could be added, with weatherboards and, later, wooden shingles popular for the exteriors.

Many traditionally trained carpenters and people living in conventional timber-framed houses pointed to the flimsiness of these basket-like structures and scornfully described them as shanties. Rightly, their views were ignored by the rest of the Chicago population desperate for housing. Balloon framing soon gained acceptance among architects and builders, and in 1865

Left The island houses on a lake in New Hampshire, USA, are much as they were when they were built in the early 20th century by the Methodist ministers and school teachers who used them as their 'summer camps'; despite being hardy folk, they retreated into town during the winter. The houses are still without running water and electricity.

Woodward's Country Homes, a building handbook in widespread use at the time, pointed out: 'A Balloon frame looks light, and its name was given in contempt by those old fogy mechanics who had been brought up to rob a stick of all its strength and durability, by cutting it full of mortises, tenons and auger holes, and then supposing it to be stronger than a far lighter stick differently applied, and with all its capabilities unimpaired.' While this view may have been technically dubious in a number of respects, it was certainly true that many balloon-framed 'shanties' were stronger than some of their cruck- or box-framed predecessors – although often this was due to inadequate maintenance which allowed moisture to accumulate in the joints and caused the wood to rot. The housing issue was a pressing concern for all of society and the lengthy debate as to the merits of balloon-frame construction was not restricted to the many architectural and housekeeping publications in circulation. The influential agricultural editor of the New York *Tribune*, Solon

Robinson, observed the ease with which houses could be built employing the new method: 'To lay out and frame a building [of traditional design] so that all its parts will come together requires the skill of a master mechanic, and a host of men and a deal of hard work to lift the great sticks of timber into position. To erect a balloon-building requires about as much mechanical skill as it does to build a board fence.' Although he exaggerates, it is true that the light components and ease of assembly contributed to the establishment of a mail-order business that was thriving by the

1850s. People in the west could purchase prefabricated houses and churches from established building companies in the east and during the 1950s, some 5,000 prefabs were made annually in New York alone to relieve the housing shortage in California. The early method of transportation varied – some went by sea around Cape Horn and others by mule across the Isthmus of Panama. As the railway network improved the houses were sent overland by train.

Although the initial attraction of this method of building was that it provided relatively inexpensive housing that was quick to

The invention of balloon framing made it possible for city dwellers and country farmers in the west to mail-order prefabricated houses and churches from the established building companies in the east.

This page and opposite The deck of pine boards is furnished simply with Skaker-inspired rockers and other country-style chairs and tables, and is perfectly positioned for an idyllic view over the lake.

assemble, by the second half of the 19th century the architectural versatility of balloon-framed houses began to be fully appreciated and exploited. Architects soon recognized that it was much easier to incorporate relatively complex features, such as bay windows, overhangs and towers, in a balloon-framed structure than it had been in traditional cruck- and box-framed buildings. In addition, the development of advanced manufacturing techniques both increased the output and reduced the cost of uniform timber, which allowed ever-larger houses to be built. It also meant that components, such as windows, doors, brackets and decorative turnings, could be mass-produced in a wide range of styles, usually at considerably less cost than their handmade counterparts. This period saw a substantial increase in the number of practising architects who, although still influenced by traditional and modern European designs, began to develop distinct American styles for an increasingly prosperous, design-conscious population who wanted better housing that would reflect their new-found status.

At least eight architectural styles became prevalent in the USA during the second half of the 19th century and up until the First World War. Most of these overlap in date and many houses were built using an eclectic combination of stylistic elements. All the styles can be broadly categorized as Victorian and, with the

At least eight architectural styles became prevalent in the USA after the mid-19th century.

exception of Richardsonian-Romanesque houses which featured rough-hewn stone facing, the one element common to all is the extensive use of timber, structurally, decoratively, or both.

The first post-Classical styles, the Gothic Revival and the Italianate, emerged in the 1830s. They were derived from the designs of British Regency houses and reflected a growing interest in the USA in historical architecture. Many early Gothic Revival houses featured irregular, picturesque plans, steeply pitched roofs and gables, castellated parapets, and windows topped with Gothic arches. Often their walls were covered with vertical, rather than horizontal, weatherboarding, which emphasized the characteristic perpendicular look. In contrast, Italianate houses featured tall, narrow windows, often surrounded by Classical-inspired architraves. They are topped with either a low-pitched roof with broad eaves supported on brackets, or a mansard roof. Derived from the 17th-century designs of François Mansart, a court architect of Louis XIV, mansard roofs gained popularity not only because their French origin lent them style, but also because

This page and opposite This weatherboard house was built by the post-and-beam method in 1985 on Long Island, in the largest pine forest in New York State. It was constructed by Timberpeg in New Hampshire and then reassembled on this site.

their generous width made it possible to incorporate a large attic storey that provided additional living or storage space.

While Classical-inspired Italianate houses were built in large numbers up until the end of the 19th century, the interest in medieval styles of architecture that had given rise to the Gothic Revival also inspired the Stick-style and Queen Anne houses. The majority of Stick-style houses were built during the 1860s and 1870s, and were broadly inspired by British half-timbered buildings. Their steep gable roofs and overhanging eaves resembled

those of Gothic Revival houses, but they differed in their characteristic decorative details, with exposed roof trusses and rafters, and raised stickwork patterns on the walls which were made from vertical and diagonal arrangements of wooden boards.

Stick style, in combination with elements taken from both Gothic Revival and Italianate architecture, provided the basis for the American Queen Anne style, which was popular from the 1880s until about 1910. In Britain, Queen Anne houses,

Above This house in Sun Valley, Idaho, USA, was designed by Mark Pynn at Darryl Charles McMillen architects. The house climbs the mountain and the vast sheets of glass break through the shingle facing to create private decks. The massive barriers were required to withstand avalanches.

designed by the leading architect Richard Norman Shaw (1831–1912), featured either half-timbering or patterned masonry. The American versions, however, boasted more complex designs and features, and made extensive use of decorative woodwork. Roofs were even steeper than on Gothic Revival and Stick-style houses, and they were often more complicated in shape with additional projections, gables, overhanging upper storeys and towers. Walls were faced with combinations of wooden shingles, elaborate brickwork patterns and terra-

cotta insets. The influence of the English designer Charles Locke Eastlake (1833–1906) can also be detected in many Stick-style and Queen Anne houses. Sturdy wooden porch posts, balusters and pendants, and an extensive use of wooden spindles for friezes and balustrades, are all features of the Eastlake style that became fashionable in the USA during the late 19th century.

In contrast to the elaborate decorative detailing of American Queen Anne houses, the Shingle-style houses built from the 1880s until around 1900 feature relatively unadorned surfaces. In most cases, their roofs and walls were covered with uniform rows of plain wooden shingles. The ornamental details were not extensive and were derived from a limited range of simple Neoclassical

elements found on American Colonial and Federal-style houses, such as Venetian windows and Doric columns. The renewed interest in early American Colonial buildings, initially expressed in the Neoclassical detailing on many Shingle-style and Queen Anne houses, led to a full Colonial Revival towards the end of the 19th century, when many copies of 18th-century originals were built.

One of the most interesting aspects of the development of this variety of architectural styles was that regional distinctions across the USA became less marked. This was largely due to the fact that most architects copied designs from the same published sources and made use of the same mass-produced building components. Similarities in designs from region to region were also fuelled by the growth of the prefabricated mail-order house business, and in the 1890s it was not unusual for pre-cut house kits to be transported by rail right across the country. However, there were not total uniformities of style as a result: the creative input of individual architects and builders meant that the

vernacular distinctions, especially in decorative detailing, survived.

In many respects the history of weatherboard timber-frame construction in the Antipodes is similar to that of the USA. Among the settlers who emigrated was a large contingent of carpenters who had been trained in traditional methods of timber-frame construction. However, until the mid-1850s in Australia, where forests were less extensive, the cost of building a timber-framed house was more than one of equivalent size in brick. The development of steam-powered sawmills resulted in a dramatic increase in the cost-effective production of the uniform wood that was required for timber frames and cladding, and weatherboard houses became economically viable, particularly when based on

This page and opposite This lodge-style shingled home overlooking the mountains of the Central Idaho Rockies was designed by Mark Pynn. The home blends forms and materials in a style common to the great lodges of America's national parks, with wood detailing reminiscent of the early 20th-century Arts and Crafts houses of Charles and Henry Greene and Gustav Stickley. The large deep-grooved shingles help to make the substantial mass of the building less apparent.

balloon-frame, rather than traditional box- or cruck-frame, construction. Despite the initial suspicion of these 'poor, flimsy, bandbox type of dwellings', the advantages were soon recognized. As in the USA, the development of a reliable railway system made it possible to transport light, prefabricated balloon-framed houses from centres of production on the coast to new settlements inland where there were fewer trained carpenters to provide the housing required. Moreover, many half-timbered houses that had been constructed during the earlier years of the century had proved ill-suited to the hot, humid climate, which caused the exposed timber frames to rot, and the advantages of applying painted weatherboards to the external walls were soon appreciated.

which often incorporated lattice screens and fretwork, was that it helped to cool the walls and interior of the house. In a country where so great an emphasis is placed on an outdoors lifestyle, the veranda became an integral part of a home, providing a shady seating area that was out of the direct heat of the sun.

Like many houses in Indonesia and southeast Asia, a number of Australian timber-framed houses were erected on wooden posts or stumps. Their purpose was to protect the house from termites and raise it clear of seasonal flooding; this allowed breezes to circulate underneath, which discouraged fungal growth and made the interior cooler. In the mountainous landscape, stumps also provided a convenient means of levelling a house into the side of a

Left During a recent renovation of this 1920s 'Queenslander' cottage, the aluminium shutters and enclosed verandas that had been installed during the 1960s were removed to emphasize space and light. The exterior joinery of the house was then painted in blue, green and white – a combination of colours inspired by the decoration of vernacular architecture in the Caribbean.

In hot countries, a covered veranda helped to cool the walls and ventilate interiors, as well as to provide a shady open-air seating area.

Adaptation to the climate also lay at the heart of three other important characteristics of Australian timber-frame architecture: the construction of bungalows and the use of verandas and stumps. Australian bungalow houses were derived from the Hindu *bungala*, which consisted of a single storey, with a tall, pyramid-shaped roof, frequently of thatch, and a large veranda on all sides. They had provided accommodation for the British colonists in India and were considered the ideal design for combating the heat and humidity of the tropics. The great advantage of the veranda,

hill. The stumps, which could easily be renewed when necessary, were often topped with a metal cap to prevent termites infesting the floorboards above. Traditionally they were treated with a mixture of tar, creosote or sump oil, and lamp black to protect them from decay. For aesthetic reasons, in suburban areas the stumps were often enclosed with stained or painted hardwood panels.

Settlers in New Zealand found a densely forested country, and until about 1890 the majority of timber-framed houses were constructed along traditional lines with mortise-and-tenon joints,

This page In this Brisbane 'Queenslander', the Australian architect Tony Suttle has exploited all the virtues of the architectural elements traditionally associated with this style of housing. An open deck at the rear and a covered veranda at the front provide plenty of space for the outdoors lifestyle appropriate to the subtropical climate, and the veranda also helps to cool the main body of the house. Additional sub-floor ventilation is provided by the garage and storage space created by raising the accommodation level on stumps that protect the house against potential flooding and rodent infestation.

rather than nailed butt joints. During the late 19th century, many balloon-framed houses of one-and-a-half storeys were built. In contrast to most two-storey New Zealand houses, in which the walls for each floor were framed separately above and below the first-floor joists, these houses incorporated studs that ran to the full height of the walls, to the sides of which were fixed the first-floor joists. Numerous timber-framed bungalows with verandas, and many English-style cottages, some of which had jettied upper floors, were also built in New Zealand in the early 20th century.

Most houses were clad with weatherboards to provide much-needed protection against the high annual rainfall, and the range of styles was extensive. Especially popular from the 1860s to the 1880s was the 'rusticated' style, where the top edges were planed to fit behind a rebate in the edge of the board above, resulting in a wall with fairly pronounced grooves that resembled channel-jointed stonework. On some grander houses this effect was enhanced with timber quoins at the corners.

This desire to pass off wood as stone was not confined to mid-19th-century New Zealand settlers. A number of American Colonial houses during the Georgian period incorporated wooden facing cut to imitate ashlar masonry – a practice that was prevalent in parts of southern England during that period. Grooved weatherboards and timber quoins were also used on several American Queen Anne and Stick-style houses during the second half of the 19th century. Yet this preference was by no means widespread, and in most cases builders of weatherboard houses have not sought to disguise the presence of wood as the primary

building material. Instead, the structural integrity and decorative versatility of wood has been emphasized and exploited to the full.

Technological developments during the 20th century have relegated the love affair with the timber house to a small percentage of the population. Yet many modern architects have incorporated wood into innovative designs of breathtaking form. For example, the modern timber houses of the Antipodes are highly regarded, especially due to the ground-breaking work of architects such as Simon Carnachan in New Zealand and Darryl Jackson in Australia, who have remained true to the concept of the plain timber house – in Jackson's case, combined with corrugated iron. They and other forward-thinking architects have exploited new materials and applied advanced engineering practices to modernize the timber-framed house beyond immediate recognition.

This page and opposite top
The design of Australian architect
John Mainwaring's pine-, plywood-
and steel-clad home in Noosaville,
on Queensland's Sunshine Coast,
is dedicated to sunlight and
ventilation. Movable glass walls,
skylights, a double-height breeze-
way, louvred windows and doors,
and an open-plan layout ensure
the house breathes and is well lit.
The wave-shaped roofs reflect the
proximity to a canal and the sea.

Opposite, bottom left to right
When designing their Auckland
home, Simon and Robyn
Carnachan employed dark-
stained timber cladding, white
joinery, clear polycarbonate and
glass to construct a series of
connected pavilions, vaults and
decks that let in the light, are
sympathetic to the local vegetation,
and allow them to feel as much
a part of the outdoors as possible.

Living with Wood

Choosing to live in a wooden house means opting for a specific way of life. In the case of the rustic log cabin and similar country-style structures, it marks a rejection of the whims of many fashionable furnishing accessories, such as patterned wallpaper and thick-pile carpet, and accepting that the interior will be dictated by the unspoken dominance of timber. Living in a room designed to emphasize the presence of wood stimulates the senses as it allows the pleasure of touching and seeing its glorious grain at every turn. Polished floorboards reflecting the sunlight, with a bold and beautiful stencilled border and a colourful, textured scatter rug; pale turquoise-painted tongue-and-groove panelling in the bathroom; skilfully carved

dado-height wall panels in the entrance hall; cathedral-like raftered living-room ceilings that soar to great heights; elegantly carved or turned balusters and stair rails are just a few of the stunning visual treats that timber offers. As a neutral backdrop for all soft furnishing accessories, wood demands simplicity by its very nature. This section examines the ways in which owners of wooden houses throughout the world have risen to the challenge. Some cultures, such as Scandinavian, and Native and South American, decorate walls and floors with images drawn from the landscape; others prefer to leave them plain, with just a simple wood stain or varnish. The decorative possibilities in the variety of treatments available is surely inspirational.

Log and Timber Interiors

The humble log cabin, once almost exclusively the territory of Alpine farmers, skiing Scandinavians and colonial pioneers, has an enduring appeal that has led to its firm establishment as both a desirable vacation house and as a permanent home. The log cabin provides a refreshing respite from the stresses of modern living and evokes an earlier way of life that seemed to be more in touch with nature and the land. The call of the wild and the romance associated with a primitive and simple lifestyle is an increasingly attractive prospect in our stressful, commercial, yet environmentally aware society. This spirit is nowhere better embodied than in America's Wild West; and while the majority of the original pioneers' log dwellings have decayed, the spirit and culture of the era in which they were built still flourish in the numerous log lodges, houses and cabins constructed and restored around the world during the 20th century. Without sacrificing the high standards of comfort and convenience that are so central to the ethos of modern society, many innovative architects and builders have relished the challenge of exploring wood's structural and decorative potential, breaking new ground in log-house design. A timber-rich interior – whether of logs or the sturdy beams of a half-timbered house – cannot help but dominate the design of the room, and the scope for creativity is endless.

Left An 18th-century Savoyard farm that was transported from the Grand-Bornand to Megève, France, and restored by the interior designer Michèle Rédélé. The salon is in the old grenier and the loft feel has been retained. The furnishings and small lamps in this living area are by the interior and furniture designer Christian Liaigre, and the theatre lantern is from Venice, Italy.

Below The front entrance to this Savoyard farm opens onto the staircase which leads up to the main living area. The forged-iron stair rail complements and contrasts with the natural wood finish. On the landing is a Colonial-style fauteuil.

Above Many of the log houses built in Alpine regions during the 18th and 19th centuries featured a number of external balconies built in at different levels. With balconies that projected some distance out from the sides of the house, carpenters would often key the sides of the handrails into the walls and then brace them inside with tight-fitting blocks of wood.

Above The fireplace in the grenier was originally in another old Savoyard house. The modern fauteuils are by Christian Liaigre and the 'manuscript' lamps on the mantelpiece are by Alexis Auffray.

The most aesthetically successful houses are those that respond well to the surroundings in which they are built, and log houses, particularly those in forested regions, appear literally to rise out of the land. Of all the vast array of architectural styles of log construction around the world, it is the colder-climate log houses that we most fondly recall, with the romance and nostalgia for a past way of life that they evoke: the Alpine chalet or the Scandinavian farmhouse, often thickly coated with snow, the American wilderness cabin high up in the forested mountains or on the open prairie. Perhaps it is because we quietly admire the triumph of practicality and creativity over the harsh rigours of a long winter where the elements are sent to test our spiritual strength. Or that we wish we still had the resourcefulness and skills of our forebears for creating superb hand-crafted objects from whatever raw materials were readily available. Maybe is it simply that, to city dwellers, log houses are a reminder that it is still possible to live closer to nature and to use natural materials to enhance the quality of our lives. At the root of the timeless appeal of the log house lies a fundamental truth: spirit of place is everything.

With this form of architecture it is easy to create a living environment where there is little change in going from the woods into a traditional log cabin. This harmonious integration of interiors with their exterior surroundings can partly be achieved by the extensive use of glass. French windows and large picture windows with panes of glass that reach almost from the floor to the ceiling not only provide extensive views over the surrounding landscape, but also create a greater sense of space and the illusion of an interior that is a part of the forest. It also ensures that the levels of daylight inside closely mirror those outside. Fuelled by the

Above The large windows are dressed with heavy jute cutains which hang from steel rings on wrought-iron spikes. The interior is simple, with 18th-century oak floorboards from the Haute-Marne region, and natural wooden walls as the perfect foil for the painted 19th-century north-Italian barometer.

invention of thermal-efficient double glazing, the extensive use of glass to bring the outside in is an increasingly common feature of modern architect-designed log houses.

In many traditional log houses the intimate relationship between the inside and outside was enhanced by the addition of covered porches, decks or verandas, which, in hot climates, served as extensions of the interior living space and, if cleverly situated, afforded panoramic views of the surrounding countryside.

Above Les Fermes des Grand Champ in the village of Choseaux at the foot of Mont d'Arbois, near Megève, are a collection of old Savoyard farms that have been restored by master craftsmen utilizing genuine antique materials from the Maurienne and Tarentaise regions.

Other important elements in log-built homes are light, space, form and function, all of which are integral to an architectural style now recognized as Scandinavian. In a historical sense, the style was also well established in northern Europe where there is a great understanding of the relationship between humans and their environment. This is reflected in their interior design, especially in their sensitive feeling for wood, and understanding followed by understatement is the key to the planning of many of their log homes. Whether the interior walls are made up of fully

Right To key the end of one log wall into the side of another, European carpenters traditionally cut square projections into the logs in the end wall, and slotted them into square holes cut into the abutting edges of logs in the side wall.

Top A large smoke canopy made from hewn logs hovers above the stone hearth of a sitting room in La Ferme du Chatel. Despite the nature of their construction, chimney fires are fairly rare.

Above left La Ferme d'Hauteluce contains many pieces of 18th- and 19th-century pine furniture from the Haute-Savoie. Log walls provided the ideal setting for rustic, provincial furniture.

Above Various forms of corner notching were used to join the ends of log walls. This is a mix of square and oval notching; other shapes include diamond and beaver (tapered like a pencil).

round, round-sided or flat-sided logs, these carpenters were expert at the various types of corner notching that could be employed in the construction, and this had a strong decorative influence on the rooms' style. It is hard to ignore such a strong architectural feature, which has become a signature of the log-house interior.

The basic plan of a log house, whether it is a simple cabin or a larger ranch-style dwelling, features a large, open-plan living room with an open fireplace. Other rooms lead off from this central area: a kitchen, bedrooms – either on the same level or on a first floor or mezzanine – and bathrooms, ensuite or separate; in a larger structure a study or a den may also be added. This plan was derived from traditional northern European cabins of hand-sawn logs that were built with a long winter in mind. The main room was the focal point of the house and was large enough to accommodate cooking pots and utensils, beds, chests and large cupboards, nearly all of which were made of wood. Also essential was a long pine-topped table with wooden chairs or a bench, and a plain, sturdy dresser in which china and glassware were stored.

Although practical use, rather than mere decoration, was the reason for an object's existence, everything was crafted with exquisite care: a food container would often feature an array of swirls and other intricately carved shapes; a tobacco box might have a simple base with a lid elaborately carved in the shape of a lion. Colour was introduced by means of paint and textiles, and

the aesthetic qualities of the hewn and scribed log walls, roof beams, floorboards and simple furniture were often enhanced with decorative stencilling, marbling and folk art. Bed, floor and furniture coverings would be changed with the seasons, with heavier fabrics used during the long winters and replaced in summer by lighter, natural linens, often with embroidered edges.

Whether in a log or a half-timbered interior, any scheme to decorate a room begins with the texture and colour of the wood on display, and the way in which the walls have been constructed. What is most impressive is the way the structural elements are rarely hidden from view behind plaster and are, in fact, a valued part of the visual design. The vast crucks and trusses of a timber frame, the massive log support posts attached to the rafters of a log-house roof, and every other visible beam, plank or rounded log has a purpose and is not just for display.

In a half-timbered interior, the choice of wallpaper or paint finish for the infill area in between the wooden framework can provide some relief from the dominance of timber. Yet in a traditional log-built structure there really is no escaping the powerful presence of the wood, and of all the forms of domestic

This page and opposite In this Elizabethan dining hall, in Brookgate on the border between England and Wales, the cruck construction and other structural timbers are left exposed and the plaster infill panels are coloured with a traditional sienna pigment limewash. The oak refectory table, chairs and benches date from the 16th century and stand on massive stone flags – the most common entrance-level flooring in houses of this quality. The sitting area (below right) is in the original sleeping loft of the single-range building built in 1350.

Whether logs are peeled, bark-on, or decorated with symbolic folk art, the visual effect of symmetry and regularity dominates a room.

This page and opposite A stunning example of folk art (rosemaling) in the guest room of a farmhouse in the Heddal Valley, Telemark, Norway, painted mainly by Olav Hansson in 1782. Hansson was one of the outstanding artists in Telemark and was particularly well known for his religious and secular painting. He was one of the small number of artists who found inspiration in the daily lives and special celebrations of ordinary folk, for example, the figure on the door. Books were also his muse, providing fanciful ideas like the elephant on the ceiling above the box bed. The cupboard was made in 1754 and painted later by an unidentified artist.

architecture, none influences the style of its interior more. Recognizing this, northern Europeans used their artistic skills during long winter evenings to create warm, colourful and inviting homes. Decorative folk art, which could depict religious or secular themes, or incorporate a charm to protect the house from evil, was an integral part of Scandinavian heritage, and often each generation would add something new to the design scheme. The natural pigment of the paint looks stunning on walls of peeled, round- or flat-sided logs, whereas fussy chintz, wallpaper borders, ornate mouldings and fancy trims would be completely out of character against the robustness of this construction. Despite the advent of modern technology, most of these early style traditions are still practised and the original concept remains: practical, simple, well-made furniture highlighted by colourful accessories.

'Every detail possessed structural significance. Extensions of log ends, coping of intersecting logs and cross bracing of poles became decorative elements.'
Andrew Jackson Downing

A sense of proportion is essential in such a dominant interior and is automatically dictated by the very nature of the construction – an insubstantial wood-veneer door or delicately carved banisters would instantly be spotted as imposters in a rustic lodge. Wood demands attention, and in a space that features vast areas of raftered ceiling, combined with the visual effect of symmetry and regularity created by the coping and chinking of the walls, with their long lines and regular curves, the decorative scheme should always complement the wood's natural beauty. The earliest log-cabin dwellers instinctively understood not to compete with this, choosing only simple, natural furniture and furnishings, drawing inspiration from their surroundings. Natural yarns were made from flax and coloured with dyes extracted from native plants, and then woven into bedspreads, chair and cushion covers, sofa throws, wall hangings, floor rugs and curtains.

European settlers took their construction skills and decorative traditions to the New World, where they explored ways to exploit the various techniques and effects they had learnt in their

This page and opposite The interior of this lodge near Aspen, Colorado, USA, shows the influence of the Great Camps of the Adirondacks, especially in the decorative bark, twig and stick-work on the fireplace (above left and centre). However, it is very much Adirondacks brought to the west. The vast scale of the log structure, with its long vistas and tremendous amount of light, relates more to western-style lodges in Yellowstone National Park, from where many of the logs for the construction were brought as standing-dead timber following a catastrophic fire. The logs were not treated, and even though they have dried out, the heat in the house causes them to settle and crack, sometimes making a sound like thunder.

room, and darker wood for door and window framing to add decoration. A ceiling could be constructed from dark rafters with contrasting pale plank lining. On wood that takes stains well, such as pine and oak, this effect can be simulated with the use of a dark-coloured wood stain.

Many early colonial log interiors were decorated with colourful images of mountain flowers and other symbols from a country left behind, but gradually local influences began to be included. In North America, the colourful decorations of the Navaho and other tribes, who drew upon their own rich culture with textiles and furnishings that take their cue from the land, were incorporated. Strong colours, such as red and yellow, blue, cream and black, representative of the sun, sea and sky, daylight and night-time, which dominate the weavings of many Native Amercian tribes, began to appear, together with the signature bold geometric patterns that are ancient tribal emblems. Stylized birds on the wing, arrows and feathered headdresses also featured widely as decorations on rugs and wall hangings.

Furniture design also took its cue from whatever objects were discovered outside, reinforcing the link between exterior and interior and illustrating the extent of the craftsman's artistry: a lamp

homeland to create homes appropriate to their new environment. Houses of hewn logs in the Midwest, west and southwest of the USA mostly feature inside walls of fully round and round-sided logs, while flat-sided logs were more often favoured in the east, as in Europe and Scandinavia. Bark was either left on the logs to enhance the rustic appearance of the interior, or peeled off for a more sophisticated look. The joints and profiles of the log ends where the walls were notched together at the corners each make a creative contribution to the room, as do the texture and colour of the wood. Builders experimented with a combination of light and dark timber to great effect, using pale wood lining to brighten a

Left *The log portion of this house in Sun Valley, Idaho, USA, was built from logs of irregular diameters using the Swedish coping method, where the bottom of each log is hand-scribed to fit the profile of the log below. The walls are constructed from 'green' unseasoned logs that shrink to fit tightly together as the wood dries out, so there is no need to apply chinking in between. The corner of a passageway leading from a guest bedroom to a bathroom illustrates a fundamental sculptural quality often present in scribed-log construction (and rarely present in the chinked alternative). Much of this is due to the manner in which the logs sit tightly on top of one another, their pure shape uninterrupted by any other material. As a result, they appear as if their curved linear forms were hewn horizontally from what was once a solid, flat-sided block of timber.*

base made from a twisted branch, smoothed and stained, its gnarled shape displayed to great effect; a sofa frame made of small tree trunks polished until smooth to the touch, designed to be seen rather than hidden under fabric; a three-legged stool made from stumps trimmed to size, its seat covered in animal skin.

As a stage for these decorative elements to be shown off to their best advantage, nothing could be better than a timber floor. Traditionally wooden floors have had a highly polished finish, but nowadays a limed effect is often applied for a more natural look. A floor made of stone or quarry tiles, softened with scatter rugs, are good alternatives, as is a natural-fibre carpet in pale brown, stone or cream. None of these flooring finishes will look out of place in a new or renovated log interior.

When a house is on more than one level the staircase becomes an important architectural feature. The more creative the builder or architect is, the more fantastic the staircase, balusters and railings can be. A wealth of new technology and materials, which contrast with the timber elsewhere in the room, can be drawn upon to create innovative staircases that curve from one level to the next or appear to be suspended in between. Some log houses feature an individual staircase full of character, with gnarled stumps and branches – even saplings – as balusters, logs as newel posts, half-logs for the treads and sawn-off logs for the risers. Combinations such as cedar sticks alternated with small half-logs for the balusters, creating a repetitive pattern, can be designed to complement the chosen interior style. For example, railings of bark-on logs are ideal for a log cabin, but may not be suitable for a sophisticated ranch house where they are usually sanded to a smooth finish. Elaborate newel posts are often created from large logs carved by artisans with patterns inspired by the local environment, depicting birds, flowers, mythical images or tribal symbols.

The fireplace, a focal point in many central living rooms, can either be located in the middle of the room, or on one wall. If it is set into a log wall, the fireplace can become a decorative feature, especially if it is made of smooth, rounded stones from a local riverbed, or built of brick with a white, smooth, plastered finish. A fireplace in the centre of a room is usually left open on both sides with a chimney rising to the full height of the ceiling. A wide timber mantelpiece provides a handy place to display artefacts,

Above and top *The vast pine log to the left of the dining area has been struck by a bolt of lightning, creating the vertical split down its length. Character logs such as these are immensely desirable to architects as they can become a stunning feature, bringing a little of the forest's history inside a room. The 'free-floating' curved staircase contrasts dramatically with the solid, linear stability of the log walls.*

Left Four gigantic columns of Douglas fir form the entrance hall of this house in Sun Valley. These logs were left standing dead for five years before being felled and were personally selected by the architect, Jim Ruscitto.

such as collections of stones, twisted twigs, dried herbs, pipes, pieces of pottery – the choice of accessories is endless with nature as the source of inspiration.

Another influential style that developed in log-house interiors and has shaped the design of many contemporary houses is Santa Fe style. When the Spanish invaded Mexico in the 1600s, two very colourful cultures were combined, resulting in an explosion of decoration. In houses of the wealthy, the flat-plank and log-beam ceilings, built in the traditional Spanish way, were made of the finest-quality timber. Simple floors, of natural stone or quarry tiles, and stone walls, painted in light tones, provided the ideal neutral background for a vast array of folk art: naïve portraits, religious symbols, tiny and ornately carved cupboards, and local earthenware, pottery and weavings. Although the walls of adobe dwellings are made of thick mud or stone, Santa Fe-style houses

traditionally feature ceilings of pine-log rafters in the style of Pueblo structures. The logs are lined with cedar saplings (*latillas*), which are usually painted white, while massive tree trunks support the ceiling and thus become architectural features. An original adobe house would have had a floor of earth, but most modern homes built in this style have stone or brick floors.

The interiors of contemporary Santa Fe-style homes are light and colourful, and filled with a mixture of Spanish and Native American arts and crafts: a Navaho chief's blanket as a wall hanging, a superb red and black lustre pot, a Cherokee woven basket – even tribal headdresses have become fashionable accessories to display on walls. Logs also make up the traditional kiva ladders, which allowed access to secret underground rooms of the same name in original Pueblo dwellings. A far cry from their intended use, these ladders are now frequently used as display frames for woven rugs – and they make great library steps.

One of the most fascinating effects in rooms where timber prevails is the way light plays on the various natural surfaces. Depending on the colour of the wood and its finish, light can bring the beauty of the grain to the surface. When wood is seen next to the whiteness of a plaster or adobe surface, the interplay of sunlight and shadow provides a remarkable kinetic display.

Contemporary architects and designers working with wood deliberately rely on the almost infinite varieties of natural colour, figuring, grain and texture of the basic building material to create

Right, far right and opposite The large living space incorporates logs, stucco, rock and glass into an efficient passive solar-heated design that is environmentally and ecologically friendly. There are 3,000 kilograms of local granite in the floors; this mountain shale, with 10 centimetres of concrete below, acts as a heat sink that stores and radiates heat. Throughout the house, walls are either dominated by the irregular but repeating pattern of the warm-coloured logs, or combined with plain, white-painted Santa Fe-style adobe portions, which break up the lines of the logs and create a feeling of light and space.

Far left *The undulating curves of white-painted adobe naturally lead the eye through the house's open-plan living areas, which are punctuated by massive log posts and crisscrossed by partial log partitions. The native granite floors and vast expanses of windows tend to bring the outside in, and the house is flooded with light.*

Left *The study area is created by the protruding end of one of the log walls, which partially encloses the space behind it. The walls are made of logs that have been cut to different lengths to appear random and natural.*

a decorative effect in their interiors, and the roughness created by the timber's primitive pit-sawn or riven finish, or the mark of an adze or plane, is all part of the interior display. Wax polish or Danish oil, and the patina of age and wood smoke are the most sympathetic treatments for interior log walls or timber beams, but thick polyurethane varnish should not be used as it prevents the wood from breathing and can give a yellow hue to the finish.

In log-house interiors around the world it has become usual to line the areas in between the solid structural posts with planks, often painted white, cream, or the traditional Scandinavian blue, creating a wonderful contrast between the smooth timber lining and the ruggedness of the structural columns. To create a visual diversity, one room may be left with the rounded posts carrying through the rough, rustic look of the exterior, while walls in other rooms, such as the bedroom and bathroom, may be panelled – partially, for decoration, or fully, for greater insulation. Sometimes this decision is influenced by the quality and quantity of the timber available, with poorer quality wood being covered by painted or woodgrained boards. The application of plank panelling enables electrical wiring and heating ducts to be hidden from

view, and also provides relief, regardless of whether the panelling is decorated or painted, from the presence of the dominant logs.

Probably the most instantly recognizable log-house interior is that of the traditional American log cabin. From its dusty prairie, hard-working origins, American cowboy style epitomizes the secret fantasy of many red-blooded Americans and embodies the spirit of the pioneer. Interior designer Thomas Canada Molesworth is credited with creating the style in the 1930s with his remarkable ranch-style Arts and Crafts furniture. He took rural man and elevated the ruggedness of his lifestyle to decorative heights. Handsome leather chairs were embellished with John Wayne-style heroes. Other chair frames were created by exploiting the natural shape of the wood, with cowboy-style fringes and metal studs as finishing touches.

Molesworth was master of the burl, described as 'an unsightly but benign tumour on a tree'. To a skilled and imaginative craftsman, a burl was like a precious jewel that could become the top of a side table or the seat of a stool. The pieces of twig and log furniture designed and made by Molesworth and his team reflected the rustic tradition found across the land. Lodgepole

A combination of traditional materials and modern technology creates innovative designs that blend into the natural surroundings.

Opposite *The golden coped logs that make up the bedroom walls provide an ideal neutral backdrop for the minimalist decoration. Their warm tones and texture act as a perfect foil for the floor and the cool white of the bed linen.*

pine and fir, chosen for their grain and stability, were his favourite timbers, which he worked into simple but effective designs. To many log-house dwellers, his design skills lay in the way he captured the romance associated with the myth of the Wild West and brought it inside the house for them to enjoy.

Molesworth drew inspiration from Native American cultures and used their more recognizable motifs – together with the cactus plant – to good effect alongside familiar cowboy images. In many respects the ways in which logs are used in Western-style interiors plays a secondary role to the furnishings and decorative details employed. Buffalo and steer heads, colourful weavings and rugs, arrowhead curtain rods and pony-skin drapes, wrought-iron chandeliers and tanned-leather upholstered chairs – hero-sized,

for real men who ate three square meals a day on the range – were regular features of his 1930s interiors and are the decorative elements at the heart of Western style. Boxes for important documents were covered in leather hide and studded; cotton cowboy scarves were framed and hung as works of art. Lampshades and cushions were also covered in hide, a shining texture to contrast with the roughness of the woven wool blankets that were used as sofa throws, patterned in typical Prairie style and edged in leather. Cowboy hats, hung on a pair of antlers, became design accessories long before the advent of the Marlboro Man and Ralph Lauren. What Molesworth did was prove to many of his peer group that you could embellish the American myth without making it too kitsch – and be successful at it.

Far left The south-western feel of this bedroom in a log house in Sun Valley is enhanced by the Native American textiles. The wicker bed and table of silver-birch branches hark back to the Great Camps of the early 20th century.

Left top and bottom The massive chinked pine-log walls lead from the entrance into the open-plan living areas. Pillars of local stone support the maple kitchen surface. The materials used are native and natural, which helps to blend this home into the rock cliff behind.

Massive logs and local rock provide a perfect backdrop for a display of colourful Native American textiles and artefacts.

Left and above The entire upstairs area of this lodge in Aspen, Colorado, opens onto the great hall below. The structure, made with 400-year-old larch that was destroyed by beetle in the 1930s, was first assembled in Montana; the components were then numbered, taken apart, and reassembled in Aspen. The massive logs cover structural steel weight-bearing plates, which allow the spans needed to create this light and airy space. The bed in the sleeping loft is made of red cedar and imported from Mexico.

Panelling

Interior walls have always been decorated in some way, and panelling first evolved in northern Europe in the 15th century as a means of draught-proofing rooms. A series of panels, known as wainscoting, consisted of thin, square or rectangular wooden boards, set in a moulded framework and arranged to cover the wall – either from floor to ceiling, or just part of the way up. As techniques and fashions changed through the centuries and craftsmen sought new media for artistic expression, panelling became ornately carved and embellished, often with moulding and dec-

Above A 19th-century fielded-panel (raised-panel) ceiling in an English manor.

Left Early 18th-century milk-painted panelling in the Simon Huntington Tavern, Norwich, Connecticut, USA, restored by Stephen Mack.

orative paint finishes. The panels provided a creative craftsman with a showcase for his art, and carved panels frequently featured motifs, heraldic symbols or a linenfold pattern – first introduced in Flanders, perhaps in imitation of curtains. Arabesques, roundels, foliage and allegorical subjects were other popular decorations, with geometric shapes created by applying battens onto the wooden boards. Panelling went in and out of vogue as alternative wall coverings were developed and in turn became fashionable, with highly decorated, painted or inlaid panelling reaching the peak of sophistication in 18th-century France. A variety of different timber was used throughout the world, with better-quality hardwood panels often left in their natural state, while those of less-attractive softwoods were nearly always painted or woodgrained.

Left 17th-century oak panelling imported into Athelhampton House in Dorset, England, from another house. Originally unpainted, the honey-coloured oak was painted brown in the 1930s and changed to its present colour in 1985.

Below 19th-century panelling fixed directly to the early Tudor brick and timber construction.

Panelling came into its own in medieval times when it became widespread in timber-rich areas, where it was often chosen in preference to the familiar plaster and limewash finish. It was also common for the framing studs on interior walls to be covered with vertical boards – if oak or fir was used the wood was normally left in its natural state, whereas a poorer-quality softwood would be painted fashionably in green embellished with gold. In the grander houses of the Tudor and Jacobean era, the panelling, usually honey-coloured or dark-stained oak, would often be applied to the dado or frieze level, or extended to the full height of the wall. Renaissance ideas, combined with a nostalgia for medieval style, resulted in an eclectic mix of Classical and Gothic decoration, with motifs such as Doric, Ionic and Corinthian columns, acanthus leaves, egg-and-dart mouldings and strapwork. Plain panels were often decorated with a carved frieze, the details of which would be picked out in coloured paint, gilding or inlay.

Right Much of the linenfold panelling at Athelhampton House was carved in the 16th century, but these panels are copies of Tudor originals and date from the mid-19th century, when the fireplace wall was totally restored.

With improving carpentry tools and skills, the panels of the Baroque era were larger and featured more expressive and elaborate carvings. Panelling began to be regarded as portable furniture that could easily be removed and reconstructed elsewhere if it was bequeathed in an estate. A trend for making lesser-quality timber appear like expensive hardwood developed, and pine or fir panels would be grained to look like oak, while oak might be treated to imitate walnut. Otherwise, wood was painted in one colour, marbled or given a tortoiseshell finish – all of which became prevalent treatments. In the grandest houses, heraldry and Classical architectural themes were often depicted, sometimes with the carved elements picked out in a contrasting colour or gilded.

Below left and bottom 16th-century oak panels adorn the walls of the King's Anteroom in Athelhampton House. The carved stone doorway is also Tudor.

Below Athelhampton House was a high-status home, and the State Bedroom featured a frieze of finely carved oak panelling which was crafted during the Tudor era. The oak tester bed and oak side table date from the time of Charles I, and the bed cover is 18th-century silk.

Living with Wood

Right The North Chamber of the Silas Deane House in Wethersfield, Connecticut, boasts an excellent example of mid-18th-century panelling. Silas Deane married into money and, as one of the wealthy Connecticut 'River God' families, he wanted to impress his neighbours with his style and sophistication. The house was built in 1766 based on French plans, but the flat-panel walls with no mantel are very typical of Connecticut. The furniture is from New England, c. 1760.

Below The colour of this simple 18th-century panelling in the Simon Huntington Tavern was carefully matched to original paint samples during Stephen Mack's restoration.

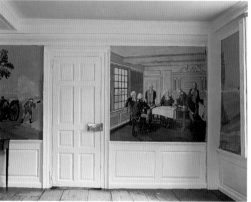

Above The panelling in the Yorktown Parlour in the Joseph Webb House in Wethersfield was painted off-white during the 1920s; in the 18th century, however, it would have been painted olive green. The pictorial wallpaper panels showing military scenes were hand-painted in Hartford, Connecticut in 1916. They are testament to the fact that, according to folklore, the Battle of Yorktown – fought during the War of Independence – was planned in this room.

Wood panelling remained fashionable as a wall covering until about mid-18th century, when tapestries, silks and cotton fabrics, stretched on battens between the dado and the cornice, became a popular fixture, and the first wallpapers made their impressive debut. After 1760 panelling gradually disappeared from the dado and was replaced by plaster, and it was not until the Victorian period that panelling was revived in entrance halls, dining rooms and studies, while living and drawing rooms were papered.

Early settlers in North America made use of many European features that they knew and loved, among them timber panelling. At first it was used sparingly, and although many better-quality houses of the mid- to late 17th century featured a fireplace wall sheathed in wooden boards, in the other rooms, especially on the upper floors, the structural framing was left exposed. Panelled dados were not a feature of American houses until the 18th century, when many elaborate rooms in the finest houses were panelled from floor to ceiling. Decorative trends from Europe were quickly adopted by colonists emotionally attached to their homeland, but there was a perceptible difference due to the harsher quality of light that makes colours seem clearer and brighter. Hence, panelling was painted in strong earth tones of yellow, almond, orange, red, brown, green and blue. Woodgraining and marbling were also used to decorate plain wooden panels.

American Federal and Empire houses often featured panelling only on the fireplace wall, or just up to the dado, with carved foliage, fretwork and gougework as decoration. Softwood panels were painted or woodgrained to look like mahogany. By the Victorian period, wainscoting of oak, mahogany and native American

Right The colours of the panelling in the Silas Deane House are interpretive rather than analysed from paint samples. The unusual carved sandstone fireplace was brought upriver from Middletown.

Below The panelled fireplace wall and half-panelling in the dining room of an 1835 house in New York State were reconstructed from an early photograph and painted in inexpensive Spanish brown, often used in secondary rooms.

Opposite and right When this early Georgian house in Spitalfields, London, England, was first built, the wall panelling would have been painted either a single colour (as in the drawing room, right), or in lighter and darker shades of one colour. Using lighter and darker tones emphasized the moulded and carved relief on the panelling – but not to the extent achieved by the splendid transfer-metal leaf gilding (gold and silver) applied by the current owner.

timbers, particularly maple and cherry, had become fashionable, either waxed or varnished. It was usual for wainscoting to extend above the dado in Arts and Crafts houses in Britain and the USA, and some featured floor-to-ceiling panelling in the entrance hall, dining room, or both. The wealthy continued to use mahogany, maple and cherry, while modest houses still featured pine or fir. Olive green, cream and ivory were fashionable paint colours.

In the Art Nouveau period, architects Charles Rennie Mackintosh and Frank Lloyd Wright incorporated vertical panelling in many of their designs, using pine stained almost black. American Beaux-Arts style was developing concurrently, and from 1870 to 1920 panelled dados were the height of chic in entrance halls and dining rooms, with the area above usually of painted plaster or patterned wallpaper. It appears that American colonists began a love affair with Classical and European styles at this time, and drawing rooms, libraries and dining rooms in the French Classical style featured wooden panels (*boiseries*), sometimes with shallow-relief decorative mouldings and ornaments in festoon and trophy designs. These were picked out in gold with a background painted white, green or blue.

Timber is a traditional feature of Scandinavian interiors. Early cottages (*stugor*) were lined with pine or fir planks painted predominantly in one colour – a slate blue-green, with grey becoming popular in the late 18th century. Yet it is the highly decorative marbled and spattered paint finishes for which Scandinavia is particularly well known. These developed as a result of the economic prosperity of the 19th century when the wealthy employed painters to decorate panelled walls with faux marble and wood-grain finishes. In many *stugor* walls were divided by a dado-style line and paint finishes were designated different areas, often with spatter painting below the dado and stencilling or folk art above.

Panelling could be plain and simple in design, elaborately carved, or made up of intricate patterns of squares, rectangles and lozenges, with either a flat or fielded (raised) surface.

From the 1920s wooden panelling was seen less on walls across the world, and where it was used, the panel was invariably plain with a wax finish. In the 1960s and 1970s architects explored the visual effect of large sheets of plywood, using them in living rooms, dining rooms and studies. Possibly this was an attempt to replicate the natural and chic Scandinavian style that was then in vogue, and it was certainly adopted by some architects in Australia and New Zealand as a simple way to cover walls. In Britain, tongue-and-groove boards were favoured more than plywood, which was seen as the poor man's building material. With the vast array of paint finishes and wallpapers available, wooden panelling is now a rare choice in contemporary homes.

Wood-lined Rooms

Walking into a room lined with wood is a unique experience because not only is the texture and patina of the timber captivating, the sensual warmth it exudes is enveloping. In many different forms, whether as fully round or split logs, hewn planks or elegantly carved panelling, wood has been a popular interior lining for hundreds of years, and of all the new materials available it remains the most versatile. Timber lining encourages its own particular decorating ethos, which dispenses with the need for endless discussion on the merits of one wallpaper over another. The fundamental decision that will influence the entire look of the interior is whether to oil, stain or paint – a personal choice, but one that often depends on the type of wood used. Whether it is in a country cottage or an elegant town house, decorating a wood-lined room can be liberating, since no formal design plan is set in motion, and, taking a cue from the wood, rough and smooth textures can be combined to excellent effect. Timber-lined walls, painted plain white or cream, can provide a neutral backdrop for a plethora of colourful decorative objects, or reflect a simple, uncluttered lifestyle which demands minimal but stylish furniture and accessories. Dominating even the humblest of interiors, wood-lined walls can be emphasized as a feature of the room with a wax finish that highlights the beauty of a highly patterned grain.

Left The Kitchen House, built on an island in a lake in New Hampshire, USA, was inspired by traditional houses on Anguilla in the Caribbean. The high ceilings of these cupcake-shaped houses accentuate the feeling of space, and the skylight situated in the sloping roof increases the amount of natural light that can enter. The simple planked interior serves as an ideal backdrop for the array of kitchen equipment.

There is no doubt that an interior clad with wooden planks has simplicity as the key element. The look and feel of the timber is pervasive, and those who grew up with this natural material – either in the country, by the sea, or in a city apartment with shiny parquet floors – cannot live without it somewhere in the house. Regardless of the choice of finish, whether wood is used to line an entire room or simply features in the form of a piece of furniture, its presence dominates an interior and cannot be ignored.

Originally, all cut timber was allowed to season naturally before it was put to use, so that the raw material revealed its qualities before the carpenter started to work with it. A piece of timber would be selected either for its attractive grain and markings, if it was to be made into a piece of furniture or panelling, or for its thickness and strength, if it was to be used as a framing

Below   These simple vertically planked interiors are from the Barfrøstua Farmhouse, built in Rendalen, Norway, in c. 1730 and relocated at the Glomdalsmuseet in Elverum. The addition of plank cladding to insulate the interior of a squared-log construction indicates the affluence of the owner.

This page The high-quality carved furniture and adornments show that this was the home of a wealthy and influential farmer. All around this room are examples of wonderful carvings, and flower and pictorial paintings. While folk art was reasonably common in the homes of wealthy farmers in this area, high-quality carving was much more unusual. The furnishings in the farmhouse date from the 18th century.

component or a support beam. Nowadays, timber is often force dried in kilns, which can dry the wood too quickly – and often insufficiently and unevenly – so when it is used, either for construction, cladding, or fixtures, it absorbs moisture in the air which can cause warping and other structural problems.

The golden glow of unpainted wooden plank cladding, naturally treated with beeswax, mat varnish or aromatic oil, creates a feeling of warmth and comfort in any room.

Timber that is left to season naturally improves over time, and working with aged wood makes a craftsman's job easier, since very often the unique nature of the piece chosen determines what it should be used for or made into, and the type of finish that will best enhance it. Indeed, many carpenters claim that an object's finished form was decreed purely by the shape, form and natural figuring of the raw material that had been selected.

When a wooden surface is not concealed beneath a decorative paint finish, with wear and tear its patina becomes smooth to the touch and its homely look is comforting. A room lined with attractive, bare wooden planks exudes an inherent warmth. Unvarnished floorboards that are polished regularly with beeswax develop a beautiful golden hue; a pine

Above The texture and colouring of natural wood characterize the kitchen in this house in Mount Glorious, Australia. Set against tongue-and-groove wall cladding, strip flooring and exposed joists, bark-on trunks support the beams and dominate the room.

Left An excellent example of simple planked walls and doors in the service area of Brookgate, a medieval manor house in Shropshire, England, restored by the architect Graham Moss.

Right and far right The Bellevue Homestead, Coominya, Australia, is maintained by the National Trust, and is a fine example of an early Australian 'Queenslander'. The kitchen's simple plank door and the horizontal planks lining the walls retain their original paintwork. The bent-wood chairs around the table are often found in turn-of-the-century Australian houses and many were shipped from Europe in kit form.

Below and below right In this chalet at Les Ferme de Marie hotel complex in Megève, France, all of the furniture is 18th- and 19th-century Savoyard. The chalets have been moved to this site from various valleys in the region and restored using old wood. In contrast to the Bellevue Homestead (right), the plank cladding lining the walls is butt jointed vertically. The door is 'double-boarded', which means it is faced with vertical planking on one side and horizontal planking on the other.

kitchen table treated with a mat varnish maintains its grain and attractive markings, as does an elm or beech chair or bench that is left in its natural state and oiled. Some types of timber are richly scented and possess an exotic, sensual quality that can be exploited to good effect and enhanced with the aroma of wood polish or wax. Similarly, a high-quality timber may be chosen for its exquisite colour and grain, which can be emphasized with the use of a natural finish. Yet even plain wood can be painted, either in one neutral shade, or decorated with stencilling or folk art in myriad patterns and juxtapositions of colours.

All parts of a room – ceiling, walls and floor – can be clad with timber planks, but these can be applied and treated differently according to their location and use to prevent blandness and uniformity within an interior. Whether applied horizontally or vertically, the planks can be simply butted together, or tongue-

A combination of wooden floorboards and plank-clad interior walls, either left natural or painted, creates infomal 'country style' homes.

and-grooved for a more sophisticated, tight-fitting finish. Ceiling timbers can be left untouched – their roughness is appealing – whereas a floor or walls of the same wood may be limed, painted, or sanded, and varnished with a glossy or mat finish. Thus, where the basic components of a room are made of the same material, a combination of treatments can be used to create visual diversity. Alternatively, plank cladding can be applied sparingly within a room to emphasize or create a design feature, such as an alcove, or a shelving unit for a collection of books.

The development of different styles of timber interiors relates to a sense of place, and within any wood-lined room there is evidence of stylistic influences from around the world that have

This page and opposite When artist Marilyn Phipps bought The Battery, on England's Kent coast, she was intent on a renovation that would create a relaxing, spacious environment for herself and fellow artists, while at the same time preserving the original character of a building built by the navy at the end of the 19th century for billeting sailors. Although some of the walls were moved to create additional and larger spaces, the plank cladding was retained and, in most rooms, repainted in the original pale 'seaside' blue. Where fixtures and fittings were required, a harmonious match between old and 'new' was achieved by hunting them down from sources contemporary to the house. For example, the heavy wooden kitchen doors were retrieved from a local post office and the wood-burning stove in the dining room is from an old cafe.

met and merged together to create a unified look. Depending on the choice of finish, this most basic and widely used building material makes an ideal backdrop for almost any furnishings, from rustic kitchen dressers to elegantly carved antique tables, to the most stark, modern stainless-steel cupboards. A combination of English country-cottage style, highly decorated Scandinavian built-in furniture, and Native American textiles and artefacts can all work well together against a backdrop of wood.

In most cases, a plank-clad room creates a less formal environment than rooms featuring more refined panelled sections, and this informality has a unique charm that is often associated with 'country style'. The term loosely applies to a casual interior which often features wooden cladding on the walls, floors or ceilings – either plainly treated with a natural finish or a simple application of paint, or decorated with split branches, moss, twigs and pine cones

to create a more rustic feel. The prime source of inspiration for rustic country style is the Great Camps of the Adirondacks. The interior walls of many of these log-built lodges were insulated with beaded or bevelled boards that were often laid horizontally so that they resembled hewn logs. The rustic appearance of the cabins was upheld and augmented with decorations, such as thin strips of birch bark between the ceiling rafters to brighten up the interiors, de-barked cedar posts and thin sheets of cedar bark and white birch bark applied around fireplaces and on chimney breasts, and stair rails of cut peeled spruce, yellow birch and cedar saplings.

'Country style' is also characterized by furniture and accessories of natural, simple textiles and materials that very often

A more rustic touch can be added to a wood-lined interior with the addition of split-log, twig, moss and pine-cone decorations.

This page The interior of this log cabin in Sussex, England, is decorated with split logs, branches and pine cones, which cleverly hide one of the main beams. The painted floor was inspired by two American quilts. Patchwork hangs on the walls and the Murphy beds are concealed in cupboards.

This page The simple
planked walls and day bed
(above) are decorated with
crochet work, adding colour
and texture to the room. The
skirting boards (left) are
made from split logs, and
the split-log ceiling (right)
has traditional moss infill.
The cabin takes inspiration
from the Great Camps in
America's Adirondack
Mountains and provides a
perfect setting for traditional
British and American crafts.

Above The interior of this tiny one-room lodge, built by the Shope family in New York State, USA, is unified and simplified by the use of pine felled on the construction site and left in its natural state.

Opposite The building was inspired architecturally by a hunting lodge in New Hampshire. The room feels large due mainly to the vast roof construction. The floor area of the lodge is about 9 metres square, and 3 metres of that is porch. The rough pine floor planks vary from 30 to 66 centimetres in width. Ample storage space is provided by the simple hollow wooden bench seating running around the walls. The solid oak chairs and stools are modern Stickley copies.

Left and above The rustic staircase with balusters of whittled cedar branches, collected by the Shope family from nearby, leads up to the communal sleeping balcony.

Right and below right The huge primal fireplace was constructed from local granite. Its harsh lines are softened by cedar branches, reminiscent of decorations in the hunting lodges in the Adirondacks.

Above The elegant dining room in this house built overlooking a fjord outside Bergen, Norway, is in the oldest part of the building, which dates from the late 17th century. The horizontally applied chamfered planks are an important clue to this date and the colour is original and typical for this area and period.

draw on a long tradition of arts and crafts, either locally made, or collected from around the world. The 'country' influence stems from our early ancestors' desire to make their basic homes attractive and comfortable, while fashioning all the furniture, tools and household objects that they required from a raw material that was easy to work with and readily available in most parts of the world.

As well as for its aesthetic qualities, timber planking was widely used to clad interior walls for the insulation it provided against the cold.

The earliest houses were just one large room where a family ate, slept and entertained around a central hearth. Ceilings were high to let the smoke drift upwards, so when the wall fireplace replaced the central hearth, there was room for another floor to be built above the entrance level. Wooden planks were the obvious construction material for these upper-storey floors, with elm a popular choice because of its hardness and its beautiful colour and grain. Before the developments of the Industrial Revolution, all wooden planks, whether they were to be used as floorboards or as cladding for exterior or interior walls, were sawn by hand and were therefore not of a standard size. Many early houses feature superb floorboards, which vary in width and often slope off in an alarming way to one side of the room. The appeal of these planks is due partly to their irregularity and also to their attractive surfaces, worn smooth and buffed to a sheen by generations of families going about their daily routine. Without these floors, much of the charm of many delightful houses would be lost.

In many parts of northern Europe and Scandinavia, where weatherboarding was traditionally applied to the exteriors of timber-framed houses to protect them from the harsh climate, wooden planks were also widely used as a lining for

interior walls to provide additional insulation. The emphasis was on practicality, and walls, floors, ceilings, doors, window frames and most other interior fittings were all constructed from wood which was in plentiful supply. As well as being an economical choice, breathable wood also provided a natural means of controlling the flow of air in and out of the house and aided ventilation.

The main dining or kitchen area was the focal point of houses and the heart of family living. It was usually a large room, with good-sized windows, a chimney breast and a wood-burning stove, which was used for cooking as well as being the most economical

Right The dining room (see opposite) leads into a later part of the house added in the early years of the 19th century. The locally made clock is painted to imitate mahogany, and the glass painting on the far wall is dated 1841.

way of heating the room. A timber-topped dining table, with either a refectory-style bench or handmade dining chairs, took pride of place. Everything in the home came from the land and, evidently, timber was not only an obvious and practical choice for house construction, it was also the most appropriate material for making

and less hazardous journey across the Atlantic meant that many families had been able to take their precious works of art, small pieces of furniture, china and glassware with them, and these initially provided inspiration for most newly crafted items. However, North America's local flora and fauna were soon incorporated into

Far left The wall of the upstairs hallway is clad with thick planks with deep chamfering, and was the original outer wall of this house built near Bergen in c. 1690.

Left The original colour of the kitchen walls was probably a darker grey than the floor, but the bright blue is also a traditional colour. The slightly beaded planks show this part of the house to be roughly late 19th century.

Opposite The chamfered planks in this 17th-century sitting room are an indication of status, suggesting that the house probably belonged to a wealthy merchant. The walls are painted deep red – a popular colour in the early 19th century.

furniture that was in keeping with the style of a wood-dominated interior. Not surprisingly, many aspects of Scandinavian and European building and interior design are apparent in the New World houses of North America and the Antipodes. Reflecting the style of their homeland, colonial kitchens of the late 18th century were wonderful, comfortable rooms that were alive with strong, earthy colours, often provided by painted floor cloths or woven flax rugs, which added texture to gleaming polished timber floors.

More Scandinavians colonized America than Australia and New Zealand, and the interiors have different characteristics as a result. Coming from a part of the world with many hours of darkness, the extensive use of bright colours, stencilling and folk art had become major aspects of Scandinavia's decorative heritage. Consequently, wall and floor treatments were more colourful in America than in the Antipodes and furniture was more highly decorated. Another reason for the differences in decorating style was the fact that European interior fashions reached the Americas long before New Zealand and Australia. In addition, the shorter

Right The plain planked wall indicates that this sleeping area for guests is in the part of the house added in the early years of the 19th century.

carvings, textiles and stencil designs; and whereas many pieces of European furniture panelling were carved with formal, but recognizable, designs such as the leaf of a tree or a classic rose, many colonial pieces depicted the airborne eagle in all its glory, or a wild, rambling native rose. Yet although the carvings and decorations that featured on American furniture were often bolder and more innovative in subject-matter, the general style of interiors was less elaborate than in Europe.

Through necessity, all objects in the home were utilitarian, and nowhere more so than in the colonies was it essential to utilize natural, readily available raw materials. Yet an ingrained respect for craftsmanship and an appreciation of first-class materials had been transported along with the pioneers' hopes and dreams for a better life, and these standards were applied to each new project they undertook. In keeping with the traditions of their homeland, mantelpieces, staircases and balustrades, and any of the other decorative components that required fine work, were made with careful thought: a balustrade would be carved, or even made from a collection of interestingly shaped branches and firmly nailed together; a mantel would be supported by corbels

Right *The hardwood plank cladding on the dining-room walls of the Bellevue Homestead shows the tripartite division of frieze, field and dado that was fashionable in the public rooms of more affluent households during the early 1870s, and remained in vogue well into the 20th century.*

carved with a leafy pattern, with inspiration invariably drawn from the surroundings – an approach still adopted by many contemporary builders and designers of wooden houses whose aim is to ensure that the interior and exterior merge with the landscape.

Whether in Europe, Scandinavia, or the New World, despite the 'country' influence and the prevalence of often quite basic hand-crafted furniture, many plank-lined interiors have a style

Above left to right *The plank panelling in this 1850s house in Rossum, Holland, was introduced by the owner and designer, Ischa van Delft. The decoration of the house is influenced by a mixture of stylistic elements, which complement each other to create a unified interior – the barometer is Swedish, the side table is from Finland, and there are chairs from Sweden and Holland. Originally a cafe with papered walls, the room has been transformed by the elegant plank cladding, which is painted in a two-tone finish, and it now evokes an 18th-century town house.*

This page The tripartite division of the walls extends to a small sitting room in the Bellevue Homestead (above), but here the cladding is painted to highlight the divisions. The horizontal tongue-and-groove planking (left) is in a covered walkway linking two sections of the house.

that can only be described as sophisticated. Vertical tongue-and-groove plank cladding was often an elegant wall covering for stylish town houses, with the long lines of the wood echoing those of tall sash windows hung with heavy drapes. In American Colonial interiors this elegance was reflected in a love affair with the Georgian, or Neoclassical, influence, which was at its height in the 1790s. Houses were more spacious, with lofty ceilings and large windows, which often extended down to the floor in the French style. A typical Federal-style dining room would feature floor-to-ceiling plank cladding painted with a pale blue-grey mat finish, a dark mahogany panelled door, a stencilled floor and a plaster ceiling. In some wealthier houses a glass-paned and painted display cupboard was built into

objects were made in the style of British furniture makers, such as Thomas Sheraton, whose designs were characterized by lightness, elegance and the extensive use of inlay, and George Hepplewhite, extolled for his ornamental, carved furniture and oval or shield-shaped open chairbacks.

Creating a welcoming home in the sometimes harsh conditions of the colonies was truly a labour of love. Many settlers had an honest belief that plain, simple things were better than anything flashy or complicated in form. Fancy marquetry and ornamentation were fine in the European cities where they originated, but in the middle of open pasture they were entirely inappropriate. Shelter had to be built quickly from whatever materials were available, so the main elements to be taken into account were function and strength – beauty and style

Opposite and above The walls of interior and furniture designer Christian Liaigre's 1830s house near La Rochelle, France, were re-clad and painted – a common practice on the island as a precaution against damp. The salon has a monastic feel, and the furniture, designed by him for the house, is Asiatic in inspiration. The fire surround has a distinctly Classical look with a hint of the exotic provided by the coral.

one wall. Many original pieces of furniture had been brought across the Atlantic by the wealthier families who had colonized the land, and carpenters with a talent for making fine pieces found their skills greatly appreciated in the New World. They became adept at creating replicas of Europe's finest furniture, many of which have become treasured antiques in their own right. Many

were still considerations, but they were not foremost. Shelving units for glassware, china and other household items were simply painted planks resting on supports that were nailed onto the wall. Early food storage cabinets were made from packing-case material and had no redeeming design features even when painted, yet they were practical and illustrate the settlers' resourcefulness.

Right and far right The vertically plank-clad walls and ceiling in this renovated and extended Brisbane 'Queenslander' have been painted satin-gloss white. Together with the flooring, windows, doors, kitchen units and soft furnishings they create a versatile white backdrop into which can be introduced vibrant splashes of colour by means of fresh flowers and plants.

Left top to bottom
A simple planked interior painted in cool whites and creams provides a blank canvas for a colourful collection of artefacts and textiles. This house on Long Island, New York, USA (top, second from top, and bottom), displays hats from Bolivia, an antique Dutch waistcoat, bags from Morocco, painted animals and flour-sack drawings from Santa Fe, and modern Donghia chairs and a table. A light, restrained interior was also created in an island house in New Hampshire (second from bottom), a region in which walls were traditionally painted in darker colours.

Opposite *In his Brisbane 'Queenslander', Australian architect Tony Suttle has created a harmonious contrast between the traditional blue-, green-, or white-painted vertically plank-clad walls and a range of modern materials, such as stainless steel and pine-veneer plywood.*

The similarities between colonial houses built in America and the Antipodes during the same period are fascinating. Many of these common features of building and design are due to the shared origins of the immigrants who transferred the traditions of their homeland to their new settlements overseas, drawing on a wealth of knowledge and decorating skills acquired over many generations to fuel their inspiration. In many cases, these influences were modified according to the climate and topography of the new environment. One shared characteristic was the appreciation of space, and this was reflected in the light, airy and uncluttered rooms that are the hallmark of houses in the New World.

Although different timbers were often employed – jarrah in Australia, kauri in New Zealand and cedar in America, with pine used in all areas – the basic house structure was similar. The American porch was echoed in the Antipodean veranda, both of which were designed to provide shade from the blistering sun; wooden louvred shutters, which helped to keep interiors cool in the summer, were another common feature in the hot regions of both continents; and in colder areas, thick, solid wood shutters built as part of the window frame became prevalent. Across the world, the colonists' movement towards the paring down and simplifying of decoration became firmly entrenched. Timber ceiling beams, chosen for their strength, colour and fragrance, were mostly left to age naturally. Window frames and doors were far from ostentatious and where top-quality timber was used it would just be stained, whereas pine planks would often be painted white.

A natural progression was the development in America of one of the most influential design movements – Shaker style. Established by the sect founded in 1747 as an offshoot of the Quakers, the Shaker influence is largely responsible for the simple, minimalist style of many contemporary interiors. A series of Shaker communities spread from New York as far west as Ohio, and from their ideals came a wish to create a uniformity of style in all the settlements. Consequently, everything had to be approved by the central community in New Lebanon. The final design of most Shaker goods was reached between 1820 and 1850, when the style's popularity was at its height, and everything thereafter was crafted to the same specifications. The Shaker creed was simple: 'Put your hands to work, your hearts to God.' Everything they

made and used was of the highest quality, and Shaker interiors were light and simple, featuring walls of cupboards and smoothly fitted drawers that are now considered to be design classics. It is hard to find a better answer to storage problems, and this makes it a style often imitated in modern, compact apartments where lack of space is a problem. Objects that might clutter a room, such as a hat, coat, tool and even a chair, were hung on pegs on the wall – an idea that has frequently been copied in many fashionable homes. Perfectly proportioned furniture, with simple, uncluttered lines, was designed with its function in mind and an abiding appreciation of the character of the timber chosen. For instance, when tiger maple or bird's eye maple was used to make the frame of a ladder-back chair, the pattern of the grain was as important as the practical shape of the chair itself. Strong colour was a feature of the interiors, with walls and furniture often painted in shades of red, blue, green and yellow. Windows were usually left bare and polished wooden floors were often covered with handmade rag or hooked rugs coloured with natural dyes. A sense of order and

Below and opposite Architect Olivier Vidal transformed this minute pied-à-terre (3 by 8 metres) in the Palais Royal in Paris, France. The walls and surfaces are covered in okoum plywood, sanded and polished to give a hint of sandalwood. The wall panels, reminiscent of the work of Charles Rennie Mackintosh, open to reveal wardrobes, cupboards, shelf units and a bathroom. The desk (below right) turns into a spare bed (bottom left), creating the feel of a ship's cabin. The only partition is obliquely angled with the desk/spare bed on one side and the main sleeping area behind (below left).

Not only can wood-lined rooms provide an elegant setting for sophisticated antique furniture, with the ever-increasing range of new veneers and finishes available, wood can be exploited for its versatility and used in combination with other materials to create modern design-conscious interiors.

calmness dominated Shaker interiors – a reminder that life's purpose was to climb the steps to heaven. The 'less is more' philosophy – the popular phrase summarizing minimalism – was a way of life for this small but highly influential community.

It is hard to identify precisely what followers of modern country style find so attractive about Shaker designs, but it is probably the absence of all the clutter and fussiness associated with Victorian English country style: floral chintz, lace curtains, and delicate china dishes, usually patterned with tiny roses or violets. Although some may consider this austere style cold and unfriendly, for those who appreciate the spirituality of pure shape and form, nothing can match Shaker style. The movement's influence is evident in the plain, uncluttered rooms of many

Right, below and opposite
The walls and ceilings of this
family retreat near Sydney,
Australia, are made of plywood sheeting (set within
steel portal frames). These
wooden surfaces, together
with the steeply pitched roof,
create a sense of living in an
Alpine ski lodge.

Above and below The guest
pavilion that 'hangs off the
edge' of the house, incorporates two bedrooms and a
bathroom, and is reached by
a covered walkway. It offers
panoramic views of the
countryside below and gives
the occupants the sense of
'sailing in space'.

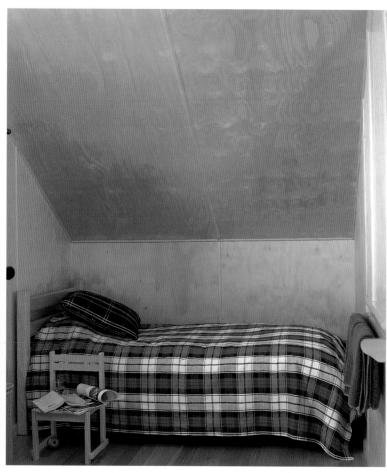

contemporary country-style houses, which feature furniture with simple lines, pure cotton bedspreads and natural baskets, often used as containers for magazines or masses of dried flowers.

Modern architects working in Australia and New Zealand are masters of the wood-lined room as a result of a long tradition of working with wood from which they have learnt techniques and drawn inspiration. Early Australian houses for the wealthy were built of sawn timber, which was used for flooring and for lining the interior walls. In the kitchens of early houses it was common to find planed tongue-and-groove boards covering ceilings and walls, or at least extending to dado height. Bathrooms were also lined with vertical planks, with the bath enclosed behind panels. When the first of many groups of British settlers arrived in New Zealand in 1840, many brought prefabricated houses with them, and others were ordered from Australia. Rough, sawn, thin boards were used for lining interiors and were fixed horizontally with handmade nails, at least until the late 1850s. These planks, of rimu or kauri, were close fitting or tongue-and-grooved to keep out draughts and stopped just short of the floor where a skirting

Opposite and right The main dining and living areas of this stunning house in Auckland, New Zealand, is divided by groups of furniture rather than partitioned off by walls. One of the fundamental design statements is the use of glass for the walls and part of the ceiling, which provides extensive views over the ever-changing landscape surrounding the house.

board was fixed in place to conceal the rough edges. By 1860, the small wooden house was established as New Zealand's vernacular dwelling, providing the basic design from which other architectural styles began to develop.

In modern Antipodean houses, architects and designers have revolutionized the style of wood-lined interiors, often by employing standard plank cladding in combination with a wide range of versatile synthetics and metals, and exploiting new technology to

Solid wall areas of painted, limed, or natural wood balance the wide open expanses of glass.

allow the incorporation of vast spans of glass. Many traditional features are still adhered to – the wood-lined bathroom is popular in renovated and newly built Colonial-style Antipodean wooden houses – but the difference is the improved techniques with which cladding is applied and the choice of stains and paints available to use as finishes. In adapting and re-creating original elements, the innovative interpretation of modern architects adds a different dimension and encourages an entirely new way of looking at interior design. Areas of timber surfaces are painted white and off-white, limed or left natural, creating solid wall areas to balance the wide open expanses of glass which let in vast amounts of natural light. In keeping with a modern, minimalist approach, plain wooden walls create a neutral backdrop for all styles of furnishings, whereas wallpapered and fabric-covered walls make strong design statements that are likely to become dated in a short time.

The way of life in the 'young' countries is less formal than in Europe and the modern timber interiors of the Antipodes and the USA reflect this attitude. Living rooms are large and open to the world through large floor-to-ceiling glass windows or sliding doors that often lead onto a wooden veranda. Inspired by Shaker style, possessions are often hung on hooks or pegs on the backs of doors and on the walls, both inside and on the veranda. Furniture is also less formal: chairs are light and portable, and large, comfortable sofas are swamped with cushions and upholstered in natural hard-wearing fabrics that will withstand the wear and tear of an active lifestyle. Where the windows are not covered by billowing fabric, timber shutters keep out the night and the occasional storm. It appears as though a full circle has been turned: despite its European origins, the style of New World interiors is now a key influence in the design of modern wood-lined rooms around the world.

Below The interior has been kept simple and neutral, with battened internal walls, tongue-and-groove ceilings and sisal matting which adds texture to the wooden floors.

Interior Details

Ever since carpenters first learned how to transform a straight piece of wood into a delicate, twisted chair baluster, there has been no end to the imaginative uses for a humble piece of timber. Centuries of changing decorative fashions have stimulated the visual senses providing inspiration and encouraging craftsmen to continue pushing beyond the boundaries of conventional design. Whether in the creation of elegantly turned balustrades and stair rails, or practical, sturdy furniture, old traditions are still followed – but with a modern interpretation. In medieval times, most free-standing furniture was made of heavy oak and elaborately carved; Shaker style, in comparison, was simple and austere. Such contrasts are what is so

fascinating about the development of stylistic trends. Each era saw craftsmen adapting and reinterpreting

designs that had been created before, bringing them into the present day. In doing so, they refined an object's

style and practicality with the kind of ingenuity that gained colonial adventurers such respect, not only from

their peers, but also from architectural historians. Many early designs were developed with the object's end

use foremost in mind, and that is what has made them classics that are still adhered to today: the clever

louvred shutter, perfect for tropical and subtropical climates because it lets air in but keeps out brilliant

sunshine; the smooth, well-turned kitchen chair; and the various configurations of shelving are just a few.

Ceilings

Before the 17th century, the structural frame of the roof served as the ceiling in most one-storey wooden houses. In cruck-framed buildings it consisted of pairs of crucks, and trusses and purlins; in box-framed structures it comprised beams, trusses, purlins and rafters. The underside of the roof covering – usually woven straw matting, wattled hazel twigs or wooden boards – was also on show. In two-storey houses, ground-floor ceilings were the beams and joists that supported the floor above, with the exposed undersides of the floorboards. The extent of ornamentation depended on the status of the building and the wealth of the household. In rudimentary dwellings, exposed joists and beams often bore only rough adze or saw marks, and in some houses the bark was left intact. However, most ceilings had some simple decoration, such as chamfered edges and stopped mouldings on the joists; more elaborate embellishments included birds, animals, floral motifs and grotesques carved in prominent positions on the exposed timbers.

In the 16th century, grander houses often had wooden beams that divided reception-room ceilings into symmetrical compartments. The earliest of these 'coffered' ceilings had a simple, grid-like appearance, and the individual compartments were either plain, or fitted with painted, recessed plastered laths. Later in the century, however, the compartments were often filled with carved timber ribs or strapwork, and where the ribs or straps intersected carved wooden pendants could be attached.

Although the various types of exposed timber ceiling continued to appear in many 18th-century log and rural timber-framed houses, by mid-17th century they had begun to be superseded in urban houses by suspended plaster ceilings. The simplest consisted of a smooth coat of plaster keyed into a network of laths nailed to the undersides of the joists, with limewash or paint applied to the plaster. More ornate versions appeared after a while in public rooms of larger houses. Initially, the plaster mouldings (including cornices) were worked *in situ*, and later, more complex patterns were made in wax or wooden moulds and then stuck into position.

Above Built in Dyfed, Wales, between 1760 and 1780, Nant Wallter Cottage has a thatched straw roof laid over a wattle hazel base. The roof is supported by log purlins and two pairs of jointed crucks.

Above right Pairs of jointed crucks and hewn-log purlins support the roof of 17th-century Kennixton Farmhouse, built in West Glamorgan, Wales. The thatched wheat-straw roof is laid over a woven straw mat.

Left The ceiling of this large 18th-century barn, redesigned and restored by Stephen Mack, is made up of 200-year-old oak roof boards, sawn on a water-powered mill, and hewn oak rafters.

Below Large de-barked log purlins support hand-hewn rafters and butt-jointed roof boards in this restored 18th-century Savoyard log farmhouse in Megève.

Left This double-floored attic in the Joseph Webb House in Wethersfield, Connecticut, USA, was the sleeping area for the household slaves. The hand-hewn purlins, rafters and planks are part of a double-pitched gambrel roof.

During the 19th and 20th centuries, suspended plaster became the most common form of ceiling, with more ornate 19th-century examples embellished with rich polychrome colours and gilding. However, wooden-board and exposed-timber ceilings did remain fashionable in many styles of housing. Notable plainer examples include the whitewashed board ceilings found in some American Federal homes, the painted plank ceilings of Australian and New Zealand vernacular buildings, and the unpainted or birch-bark-lined boards found on ceilings in the Great Camps of the Adirondacks. More elaborate examples appeared in Italian Renaissance Revival houses, which had deep coffered ceilings incorporating central rosettes and carvings embellished with gilding and red and blue paint. Many Spanish Colonial Revival houses also had coffered ceilings, but these were plainer and the timbers were usually stained dark oak or mahogany. Similarly, most Arts and Crafts houses on both sides of the Atlantic had chamfered

Above left In the guest bedroom, wooden pegs cover the steel strengtheners in the constructional wooden frame.

Above right The Arts and Crafts style is continued with the solid, square-shaped oak furniture. Even the windows are designed so the sunlight shining through reflects a grid pattern that is repeated on the ceiling and echoed throughout the furniture in the house.

Above and right In this lodge-style home in Sun Valley, Idaho, USA, architect Mark Pynn has developed a unique wooden roof system with a grid-like 'structural lattice' ceiling, made up of double and fake purlins. This served as the basis for the Craftsman-style detailing which is found throughout the house. The Mission-style geometrically shaped light fittings are characteristic of the Arts and Crafts movement.

beams augmented with ribs, bosses and moulded pendants, although grander houses in this style often had barrel-vaulted ceilings incorporating musicians' galleries.

During the 20th century, notable exceptions to the plastered ceiling include the tongue-and-groove boards (mostly varnished or painted pine) that have been installed in numerous styles of houses, particularly in kitchens and bathrooms. But the most significant development over the last 30 years is the revival of pitched roofs (often abandoned in favour of flat roofs during the Modernist era). This has allowed contemporary architects of log, timber-framed, and even stone and brick-built houses to explore again the visual dynamics of exposed skeletal roof structures.

Right In his 1830s house near La Rochelle, France, designer Christian Liaigre combines his love of bleached, light-coloured oak floorboards, and white-painted plank cladding and simple beamed ceilings with the contrasting textures of oily hardwoods.

Below In this mountain house in Sun Valley, the chimney stack of local rock contrasts with the simple maple ceiling beams.

Bottom The beamed ceiling in the living room of this house in Rossum, Holland, exposes the underside of the floorboards of the storey above.

Floors

There is nothing quite like the effect of a highly polished wooden floor to enhance the decorative scheme of a room. Depending on the timber used and the choice of treatment, wooden floors provide the ideal backdrop for many styles of interiors, and complement antique and contemporary furniture alike. The colour and beauty of the grain cannot be denied, especially if the planks are merely coated with oils for protection; too much shine is counter-productive and it is wise to remember this when choosing a finish.

When early lofty houses were divided into more than one storey by the insertion of a ceiling, the timber floor came into its own. Prior to that time, most ground-level floors were of beaten earth, with flagstones or slate paving also common, although a formal room, such as a parlour, often had a wooden floor. Once

Below left Bright-yellow painted floorboards in the bathroom of a modern extension to the early 19th-century Burr Tavern, in East Meredith, New York, USA. The white-painted Victorian tin bathtub is oak-rimmed.

Below right White colourwashed floorboards, finished with clear satin-gloss varnish, are co-ordinated with the walls and furnishings to create a cool Caribbean-style interior in this 1920s 'Queenslander' in Australia.

Bottom right Bleached floorboards and white-painted plank-clad walls and window shutters establish a '1930s seaside-holiday-home look' in Christian Liaigre's 1830s house near La Rochelle in France.

Right Stained and varnished wooden floorboards, which are practical and easy to keep clean, contrast with the white-painted tongue-and-groove wall cladding in this 1920s house built on an island in New Hampshire, USA, creating a light, airy interior.

Below and bottom The floorboards throughout this 1980s house on Long Island, New York, are butt jointed and made of locally grown pine. In the dining area the pine has been clear-varnished to show off the natural colouring and figuring of the wood. Elsewhere, however, many of the floorboards were treated with what the owners describe as 'driftwood grey' colourwash.

the upper-storey timber floor made its debut, there was no doubt that it would become a stylish feature of any house. Elm was preferred to oak due to its hardness, its attractive grain and its light colour. All early floorboards were sawn by hand, and as a result they were of different thicknesses and widths, giving floors in older houses an individual charm that is far more full of character than floors of modern, standard-sized machine-cut floorboards.

Ready-cut planks of red and white fir, known as deal, were being imported into England from Scandinavia by the 17th century, and these materials became a cheap alternative to solid oak and elm. The intriguing aspect of these early floorboards was that they were not fixed to the structural frame, making them a

Left Stained and waxed butt-jointed wooden floorboards in a parlour in Stephen Mack's 18th-century, one-storey 'Cape Cod' house, Chase Hill Farm in Rhode Island, USA.

using a variety of different-coloured timbers, which they laid in elaborate patterns designed to create illusionary effects. A cheaper alternative was to paint or stencil a pattern directly onto the floor, either all over, or just around the edges of a room. Inexpensive rag-strip rugs were a typical floor covering even then.

Machine-prepared tongue-and-groove boards of an even width were introduced in the 1820s and the floor was fixed onto joists. In the distant colonies of Australia and New Zealand, timber flooring was much in demand, and native hardwoods such as kauri and rimu were sawn, planed and polished. Stripped pine boards, sometimes stained a darker shade, also covered many floors in the New World. The most important thing was to make the floorboards gleam, creating a stunning backdrop for the furniture and soft furnishings.

A modest English Victorian house would have had plain, wide floorboards covered with large rugs. The edges of the floor were stained and polished with beeswax and turpentine, or made up with parquetry. In the USA, pine boards were commonplace until the Arts and Crafts

portable feature that could be removed should the house be sold. Until the 17th century woven carpets and rugs, imported mainly from the eastern Mediterranean and the Orient, were expensive and rare. Before then, mats of rush and straw were commonly used as floor coverings, especially in less formal rooms.

Wooden blocks were a feature of floors in grand houses by the 18th century. Craftsmen developed parquetry skills, often

period, when the American architect Gustav Stickley recommended that wooden floors should be as dark as the adjacent wall panelling. Oak, maple and other exotic hardwoods were then favoured, with the finest wooden planks cut from the full width of tree trunks. Art Nouveau floors were usually of smooth, polished timber, since this formed the ideal background for the patterned and colourful carpets and rugs that were a major feature of the

Wooden boards are the most basic type of flooring, but their natural beauty can be exploited to complement and enhance many design schemes.

Right By mid-19th century, floorboards were being cut narrower and to a more uniform width than they had been been in previous centuries. However, the boards in this 1850s Dutch house are over 30 centimetres wide – about 30–50 per cent larger than standard.

Left Built in 1873 by the British navy, The Battery once served as accommodation for sailors training in Whitstable, Kent, England. It is floored throughout with thick pine boards, which have been stained a red-brown mahogany and coated with gloss varnish. Appropriately, they resemble the deck of a ship.

Left Greatly admired for its excellent durability and its red and brown tones which give a feeling of warmth to the room, Tasmanian oak strip flooring was chosen for the combined kitchen-living-dining area in this family weekend retreat south of Sydney, Australia.

style. Waxed or polished oak or teak floorboards were used in grand Edwardian homes, but pine tongue-and-groove boards were more common in the average house, with herringbone-patterned parquet floors making an appearance in suburban living rooms, kitchens and passageways – a trend that crossed the Atlantic during the American Beaux-Arts period.

By the 1920s and 1930s a parquet floor of light-coloured wood was standard. The patterns ranged from simple herringbone to complicated geometric designs, a fashion that continued throughout the 1960s as an alternative to dark polished hardwood boards. In some houses, most of the floor area was covered by a patterned carpet and the wood effect was relegated to the border. Hardwood block-and-strip floors remained popular despite the rapid growth in popularity of alternative flooring materials, such as linoleum, in the 1950s. With the mushrooming of converted warehouses and loft spaces that occurred throughout the 1980s, wooden floors became increasingly popular, sometimes with stencilling around the edges. Easy to clean and maintain, and complementing any interior style, bare wooden floorboards have an enduring appeal.

Stairs

The simple ladder naturally evolved into a straight flight of stairs, often fitted into a narrow space and partitioned off. Dog-leg staircases, consisting of two flights at right angles with a half-landing, were also common as they took up a small amount of room. Grand Tudor and Jacobean houses had lavishly decorated staircases, and even newel posts in average houses were turned and carved. A spiral staircase with a large square central newel post of brick or stone was the ultimate in chic, but by mid-16th century it had evolved into the framed newel stair – a timber-framed tower surrounded by a brick or stone stairwell. Elizabethan balusters were turned to look like columns, or waisted; carved and pierced flat balusters were typical of the Jacobean era. Most staircases were 'closed string', with the balusters set on a diagonal brace rather than on the stairs themselves, creating a straight rather than a stepped profile. Baroque staircases were massive and usually of oak; the finest featured balustrades of continuous pierced panels depicting strapwork or acanthus scrollwork, sometimes with carved figures. Turned, waisted balusters were common until about 1650, when the vase shape was favoured, and after 1660 twisted banisters were popular. Georgian houses often had a main

Below left and right The treads of this staircase in a house in Aspen, Colorado, USA, are made from peeled logs, cut from standing-dead 400-year-old larches killed by beetles or fire during the 1930s.

Bottom left and right Whittled cedar branches serve as the balustrade and small skip-peeled cedar logs are used for the handrails in this Adirondacks-style staircase in a one-room Stick-style cabin in New York State, USA.

Opposite The splendid staircase in this house near Biarritz, France, dates from c. 1770. It is sawn and carved to a flatter, rustic version of a more refined, rounded Louis XIII pattern.

Below The balustrade of this spiral staircase in a lodge in Aspen, is made of bark-on branches; it turns around a massive central newel post – a standing-dead tree trunk from Yellowstone National Park.

Above left *A plain quarter-turn staircase in the c. 1715 Buttolph Williams House, in Wethersfield, Connecticut, USA. The handrail of a boxed-in staircase often ran along the external wall, but here it forms part of a short balustrade.*

Above right *A narrow stair hall, featuring maple treads and risers and a maple handrail, leads from the dining room to the kitchen in this modern house designed by architect Mark Pynn and built into the side of the mountain in Sun Valley, Idaho, USA.*

Right *A boxed, open-string, dog-leg staircase at Stephen Mack's home, Chase Hill Farm, built in the late 18th century in Rhode Island, USA. The risers, under-stairs door and tongue-and-groove planking are painted Colonial red.*

staircase and backstairs for servants; apart from the polished handrail, the wood was given a flat-colour or woodgrain finish. By the early 19th century most staircases were 'open string', with tapering balusters fixed into the exposed treads; handrails were flatter and ended in a smooth circle on the newel post. In Regency and Victorian England handrails were often mahogany, and fancy turned balusters and newel posts were mass-produced. The 1930s saw cantilevered staircases following the line of curved walls, yet it was not until the 1950s that architects realized how staircases could open up an area. Bare wooden stairs have regained popularity as they are easy to maintain and are also in keeping with the prevailing design philosophy that advocates simple, clean lines.

Left and far left *A double-dog-leg open-string staircase in the Silas Deane House, built in 1766 in Wethersfield. The highly polished mahogany balustrade, which was produced locally in Wethersfield, has a repeated pattern of two different styles of turning – a fairly common feature of later Colonial designs. The profile of the handrail is also typical of the mid- to late 18th century. Considering the extent of ornamentation in the treatment of the balusters, the tread ends are relatively plain.*

 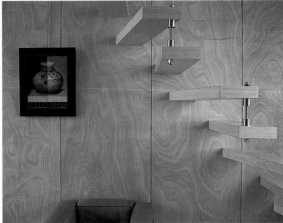 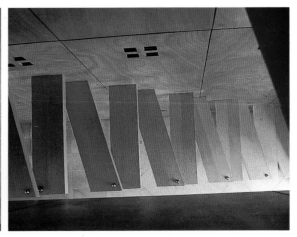

*Above, **left to right*** This unusual banister-less staircase, designed by the architect Olivier Vidal, creates a feeling of lightness and space in this compact apartment in the Palais Royal, in Paris, France. Bolted together in pairs with chromed steel fittings, the solid ash treads, arranged in a zigzag pattern ('Leonardo da Vinci-style') are cantilevered into a wall clad with sanded and polished okoum plywood.

Above The stairwell in an 1830s house near La Rochelle, France, retains its original paintwork, but has lost its simple balustrade.

Left The stairs in the early 19th-century Burr Tavern, in East Meredith, New York, were originally painted chrome green, but were subsequently stripped. The current owner has repainted them yellow ochre, olive green and vermilion.

141

Doors

An external door provides a focal point from which to design the architectural style of a facade and is a feature integral to determining the look of a building. Equally, the design of internal doors influences the proportions of the rooms, and the choice of

Whether it leads into the elegant entrance hall of a town house or a simple cottage kitchen, a door can make a stylistic impact.

  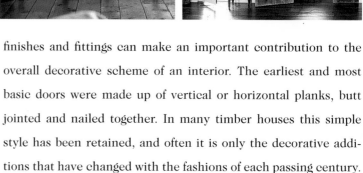

Above left and centre Prior to and during the 16th century, most doors were made from butt-jointed vertical planks (usually oak) secured on the reverse side with horizontal battens. These doors from Brookgate, an English timber-framed manor dating from the 14th century with 16th-century additions, are typical examples – although the one on the left is original, while the one on the right is a relatively recent replacement.

Top right A sturdy, double-boarded (or cross-boarded) unpainted pine door, in Stephen Mack's restored late 18th-century Chase Hill Farm in Rhode Island, USA. The heads of the nails that secure the boards together are left exposed – a decorative convention that dates back to the Middle Ages.

Above, left to right An 18th-century forged-iron door latch; panelled doors hung on hand-forged iron H-hinges; and a pair of plank doors made from wood salvaged from the original structure – all in an 18th-century barn in Harvard, Massachusetts, USA, designed and restored by Stephen Mack.

finishes and fittings can make an important contribution to the overall decorative scheme of an interior. The earliest and most basic doors were made up of vertical or horizontal planks, butt jointed and nailed together. In many timber houses this simple style has been retained, and often it is only the decorative additions that have changed with the fashions of each passing century.

In Tudor times, external doors were made from oak planks, which could be up to 65 centimetres wide. These were either held

Below A highly polished wide-plank oak door, made during the 16th century, leads into a bedroom at Brookgate. The only concessions to decoration on the reverse of the door are the chamfered edges of the cross battens, the latch and hook.

together by horizontal battens applied to the inside face, known as a cross-battened door, or by a second set of planks laid at right angles to the first – a double-boarded or cross-boarded door. The heads of the nails were frequently left on display as decoration.

Linenfold panelling, so called because the wood was carved in such a way as to imitate folded fabric, was fashionable on internal doors of the mid-16th century. Occasionally grander internal doors were made up of a wooden framework with an infill of

Above All the doors in the early 19th-century Burr Tavern, in East Meredith, New York, USA, are old and were installed by the present owner. This rustic two-plank cross-battened door displays its original buttercup-yellow milk paint, and the more formal four-panel door was recently painted olive green.

Above A fielded-panel (raised-panel) door with an unpainted iron bean thumb latch at Stephen Mack's home, Chase Hill Farm. The door, painted in a soft shade of blue, looks striking against the authentic-looking flaking white-wash that has been applied to the plank wall.

Opposite top Originally papered, the walls of this mid-19th-century Dutch house were subsequently plank-panelled – with old and new wood – and painted. The panelling incorporates a 'hidden' door, which is faced to match the design.

Opposite bottom This four-panel door within the vertical planking of a sliding wall is in an 18th-century barn which was moved and redesigned by Stephen Mack.

Left The 17th-century panelled walls and doors in the dining room of the English manor, Athelhampton House, are made of oak and were painted in 1985.

Below A half-glazed panel door, designed to maximize light on a staircase in the 18th-century Simon Huntington Tavern in Norwich, Connecticut, USA.

Below right A pair of large half-glazed doors – painted coral to reflect the proximity to the sea – divide the entrance lobby from a sitting room in Christian Liaigre's house near La Rochelle, France.

timber panels, but the majority were cross-battened doors. Internal doorways were generally more elaborate than external door frames, with Classical-style details such as pillars and cornices featuring after the mid-16th century. Primitive but effective strap hinges were usually employed, either sunk into or nailed onto the door jamb. Individuality could be stamped on a plain timber door by the type of latch fitted: normally doors had simple latches of iron or wood; wrought-iron or brass box locks were luxuries that were only seen on doors of grander houses.

Panelled doors were a feature of Baroque houses, with between two to five panels per door in a variety of shapes and mouldings. By that time, hinges were mounted on the door face rather than being cut into the inside edge as previously. With the progression of society, a box lock was not only necessary for security, but became immensely fashionable and was often ornately engraved, providing another creative outlet for artisans. By the mid-18th century, English interior doors featured drop handles and the ubiquitous door knob was created. Internal doors had plain-rimmed brass or iron locks, while wealthier house owners sought brass or gilt patterned locks.

In North America, two-panel doors in low relief were common in quality houses of the late 17th century. By the 1730s fashion dictated raised-panel (fielded-panel) doors with classical surrounds, the influence for which was drawn from imported pattern books and from European traditions introduced by immigrant

become fashionable to paint door panels decoratively in the style of Pompeiian and Etruscan work, and by the beginning of the 19th century Egyptian motifs, inspired by Emperor Napoleon Bonaparte's military campaigns in that country, were popular among the rich. This was also the era of the brass push plate, or finger plate. A notable feature of the Regency period up to the 1840s was the introduction of tall double doors dividing the front and back reception rooms. Doors had either four or six panels with mouldings; and imitation rosewood or flame-mahogany woodgrain finishes were popular. Iron or brass surface-mounted locks, or newer cut-in mortise-type locks were used at this time.

During the Victorian era, internal doors to rooms that were used for entertaining could be up to 8 centimetres thick, with a number of panels and mouldings, whereas doors leading to every-day rooms were often just 2 centimetres thick. Woodgraining remained a popular finish for ready-made pine doors, and sliding doors between the parlour and dining room were a common feature of American Victorian houses. In both English and American Arts and Crafts houses plain plank doors, inspired by medieval style, came back in vogue, with iron latches rather than door knobs. Some painted door panels of the Aesthetic Movement of the 1880s feature flowing native floral and bird designs, and door furniture was fashioned from beaten copper.

craftsmen; a common pattern was a broken, segmented arch with a pineapple finial. Some internal doors had louvred shutters which served as screen doors during hot summer months.

The internal doors of the more modest houses of the early 19th century were of painted deal, but the grandest internal doors were of solid mahogany with polished panels framed by incised ribs or beaded moulding. Plain doors could also be grained or painted, while ebony, holly or cherry-wood inlays were widely used to add a touch of the exotic to a door. From the 1770s onwards it had

Right *The six-fielded-panel entrance door of the Burr Tavern is fitted with an iron latch; in rural areas, brass fittings were usually confined to internal doors during the early 19th century.*

Far right *Restored by Stephen Mack, these doors have brass box locks, which were most popular after 1725 for those who could afford them, but were out of vogue by the end of the 18th century.*

Top left and right These are fielded-panel doors in Stephen Mack's home, Chase Hill Farm. In urban areas, the six- rather than the four-panel door became increasingly common in Georgian houses during the course of the 18th century. The degree of relief on the panels also changed during this period, from heavy and deep to relatively light and shallow.

Above left A ten-panel arch-top door, flanked by Classical pilasters, in the Federal-style parlour of the Joseph Webb House in Wethersfield, Connecticut.

Above The six-fielded-panel door, with brass furniture, is typical of late 18th-century Georgian rooms on both sides of the Atlantic.

Polished teak or mahogany doors added a stylish feel to many English Edwardian houses, and softwood doors were painted to match the decor of the room.

As building techniques improved, doors in kitchens and service areas were framed, ledged and braced. American Beaux-Arts houses were expansive, with wide open archways linking entrance halls and living spaces. Mahogany was popular, as were French-inspired door panels painted with floral themes, Classical trophies and romantic landscapes. Stylized Tudor-style linenfold panelling was common in 'Tudorbethan' houses of the 1920s on both sides of the Atlantic, but after the 1930s, mass-produced plain pine doors were prevalent. Plywood doors with no panelling or moulding were seen as the way forward by Modernists, until architects recognized the role of a door in defining the symmetry of a room, and the uniqueness of wood's decorative and design potential was again exploited to the full.

Windows

A window is much more than a means of letting light into an interior. Its location is an important factor in determining the layout of the furniture, and in most rooms the window is a focal point. Therefore, the type of timber chosen for use in a frame

wind and rain. Later, lattices of small glass panes were fixed directly to the mullions or into wrought-iron hinged casements.

Glass was readily available from the late 16th century, but its high price meant that in domestic architecture glazed windows were an option only for those building the grandest of town houses and farmhouses. Early glass, known as crown glass, was

Below An upstairs chamber in the 1678 Hempstead House, New London, Connecticut, USA, has original casement leaded windows with diamond-pattern cames fixed to iron standards (vertical rods).

Below right Diamond-pattern cames fixed to iron standards at the Buttolph Williams House, c. 1715, in Wethersfield, Connecticut. Unlike the casement windows (below left) these do not include a section that slides into the wall.

becomes as essential as the view from it. Whether the window frame is painted or not, wood lends a room a certain character that no other material can provide.

A sense of proportion was of paramount importance to the planning of a room's layout, and the shape of a window responded partly to tradition, partly to fashion and partly to the dimensions of the space that was to be lit. Until the late 16th century a window, or light, was merely an unglazed opening in the wall divided by vertical wooden posts (mullions), sometimes with horizontal wooden bars (transoms). Most windows had internal hinged or sliding shutters of solid wood to keep out the

Right Two 12-over-12 sash windows allow plenty of light to enter this attic bedroom at Stephen Mack's 18th-century Chase Hill Farm in Rhode Island, USA.

Right These 12-over-12 sliding sash windows in Chris Ohrstrom's Burr Tavern in East Meredith, New York, USA, have been painted in Spanish brown. As the pigment was locally available, this was an inexpensive colour which was traditionally used on joinery in secondary rooms during the late 18th and early 19th centuries.

Above and top left The sliding 'Indian' shutters in the 18th-century Isaac Stevens House in Wethersfield were designed to block out light and provide privacy and insulation – they could also be closed if the house was attacked.

Above right A classic eight-over-eight sash window in The Battery, a late 19th-century timber-framed building in Whitstable, Kent, England, is painted a pastel pink-red to contrast with the pale-blue plank cladding.

Louvred wooden shutters lend an ordinary window great versatility, providing ventilation, but shielding the interior from direct sunlight.

Left The bi-fold internal louvred shutters in the Bath House, a modern extension to an early 20th-century wooden house on an island in New Hampshire, USA, were made by the owner.

Right Also in the Bath House are vertical louvres set into a slit-trench window. Louvres such as this can be fixed or designed to swivel.

cut from blown discs and was very thin and dull. The individual panes, which were called quarries, were arranged diagonally. By the 17th century glass panes were larger and usually arranged in rectangles. Not all windows could be opened, but if they did open it was by means of wooden casements hinged to wooden mullions.

During the Baroque and Georgian periods, windows became larger and more elaborate. The development of counterweighted vertical-sliding sash windows in the 1670s meant that mullions and transoms were no longer needed, which allowed larger areas of glass that could be opened. Sash windows became fashionable in grander brick houses, but in timber-framed houses, casement windows with glazing bars were still used. Both Baltic fir and pine were popular for window frames, which were protected against the elements with white lead paint. Where internal shutters were

part of the window design, the outer faces and the wooden surround were usually panelled to match the rest of the joinery in the room. It is not uncommon to discover original shutters coated in layers of white paint – a treatment that is acceptable in a contemporary design scheme, yet one that hides the true beauty of the pine's grain and golden colour.

Late Georgian houses were filled with light, with windows on upper floors nearly always as tall as those on the ground floor. Drawing-room window sills were placed at floor level, which gave the room a feeling of spaciousness and elegance. In the 1780s, another stylish development in window design was made in the form of French windows, which allowed easy access into the garden or onto the small balcony of a town apartment. French windows create a sense of drama in a room and remain an enduringly popular architectural feature. During the same era, variations on the conventional sash window began to appear, with round-headed openings set in arched or rectangular sash frames and Gothic-style windows becoming popular.

Opposite Because it has been positioned high up on the Bath House's plank-clad wall, the louvred trench window admits daylight while ensuring the privacy of the occupants from the outside.

By 1840 glazing bars had become thinner and the bay window had pride of place in front rooms, while shutters were less popular. In Britain, the abolition of window tax in 1851 and gradual improvements in glass-making techniques allowed windows to be stronger, larger and cheaper by the early 1900s. The heavy exterior façades of early Arts and Crafts houses were broken up by the random arrangement of vernacular wooden casement windows with small leaded panes. Devotees of the style placed a great emphasis on the value of light and air in interiors, and elongated sash windows became popular in Queen Anne houses. Bay and oriel windows (second-storey bays) were prevalent in England, while rows of windows were popular on both sides of the Atlantic. Following the example of the innovative work of Charles Rennie Mackintosh and Frank Lloyd Wright, windows were either set flush with the wall surface or recessed without the traditional exterior surround.

The Scandinavian influence made itself felt in England during the 1930s and timber again became a favourite framing material. Vast picture windows – invisible barriers between the exterior and interior – were popular among Modernist architects. In a secluded rural house a picture window could provide an expansive view of the landscape and greatly enhance the property's value, but in a city it often left the occupants feeling exposed and vulnerable.

Traditionally, wooden window frames were protected from the elements with paint or varnish, depending on the timber used. Pine was the obvious choice as it was cheaper than more desirable hardwoods, but as sealant technology has developed, varnished hardwoods are now used over poorer-quality pine frames – partly for aesthetic reasons and also because they require less maintenance.

Above As well as admitting light to the upstairs balcony and the top of the stairwell, these rectilinear wooden casement windows were deliberately designed, by architect Jim Ruscitto, to contrast with the curvilinear log wall.

Above Corrugated tin is not used only as a roof covering: in this Australian house it serves as metal facing, painted white and accommodating two casement windows.

Above A combination of casement windows and adjustable louvres is very adaptable, and thus well suited to the vagaries of Brisbane's subtropical climate.

Above and above right The artist's studio, in an Australian house designed by architect John Mainwaring, is well served by a wall of adjustable glass and louvred shutters. They are topped by large fixed panes of glass, which continue to admit natural light when the louvres below are shut for privacy or insulation.

Above The insertion of a series of large panes of glass in one of the gable ends of this house in Aspen, Colorado, USA, ensures that plenty of natural light illuminates an upper storey open to the Great Hall below.

Left and below The entrance corridor extends through two storeys in a house designed by architect John Mainwaring in Queensland, Australia. Adjustable casement and louvred windows allow the entry of natural light to be controlled and ensure good ventilation and an even air-flow so air-conditioning is not needed. At ground level the corridor can be opened to the outside by means of retractable shutters.

In hot climates, the placement of windows is crucial to create living spaces with sufficient light, but at the same time to provide much-required protection from the damaging effects of direct sunlight. Timber-framed skylights located in the roof; long, thin windows placed high up in an outside wall; and wooden louvred shutters are just three effective solutions which provide light and ventilation, but protect furniture and upholstery from the sun.

As contemporary architects explore the endless design possibilities that the combination of glass and wood offers, and as ever-improving technology allows thermally efficient glass to cover even greater surface areas, timber-framed windows will continue to be a strong feature of domestic architecture.

Built-in Furniture

Fitted furniture was common in early 16th-century Europe and Scandinavia, and the kitchen and dining room were obvious places in which to build storage units. Ventilated food cupboards have always been a natural, practical way of keeping food fresh and many country properties still incorporate such a cupboard, usually with a fine mesh covering to keep out insects. Storing food under lock and key in wealthier households meant that many built-ins featured ornate iron fittings. Most kitchens had what was known as an aumbry, an enclosed piece of furniture created by attaching a frame and doors to a recess in a wall. Some inventories from the 15th and 16th centuries suggest that its primary use was for storing books, while others indicate that it was a wall receptacle for leftover food to be distributed as alms to the poor. Many aumbries were located near the fireplace to keep the contents dry, and they varied in size depending on the wealth of the household. Other early kitchen cupboards, some of which had internal partitions, include bacon cupboards and corner cupboards. Popular in the Baroque era, corner cupboards featured shell-head decoration and curved shelving, and, in Scandinavia, folk art paintings.

Until the end of the 17th century, most Scandinavian interiors featured built-in furniture – walls were honeycombed with beds that were carved and prettily painted. Panelled rooms of the 18th century often had an alcove built into a corner with tiered

> From its early 16th-century origins, practical, built-in wooden furniture has become a standard element in many compact homes.

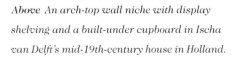

Above An arch-top wall niche with display shelving and a built-under cupboard in Ischa van Delft's mid-19th-century house in Holland.

Left Panelling in the Dining Parlour of the Issac Stevens House in Wethersfield, Connecticut, USA, incorporates a cupboard for china – a typical 18th-century feature.

Right and above right An elegant, Neoclassical-style, arch-top wall niche, flanks a fireplace in the Joseph Webb House in Wethersfield.

shelves for displaying china, known as a buffet. Shallow hanging wall cabinets were made during the middle years of the century. They were frequently made in pairs and nearly always glazed. A chimney breast in a panelled room was usually flanked by hidden cupboards for storing logs and pine cones. Corner cupboards had become a familiar fixture and, with the development of glass panes, they offered a creative opportunity to display ornaments. Seats fixed in window recesses and in areas close to open fireplaces were popular, as were built-in settles with hinged seats to provide storage space. As more books were published, many houses

Above Built-in bookshelves accommodate the pitch of the roof in this attic room in a post-and-beam house on Long Island, New York, USA.

Above These pine bookshelves follow the contours of the hexagonal-shaped Bath House, in an island home in New Hampshire, USA.

Left A painted built-in dresser – a typical piece of 18th-century furniture – stands in the kitchen of the Silas Deane House, built in Wethersfield in 1766. At one stage the lower section of the dresser may have been enclosed by doors.

shelves of oak or elm were built into the housekeeper's rooms or on the walls of upstairs corridors to store linen. One of the more ingenious Scandinavian designs of the 18th century was the plate rack, attached to the wall for displaying heirloom pottery tureens and the like, and now a standard feature of many kitchens.

By the early years of the 19th century Neoclassical taste dominated fitted furniture, and high-quality polished hardwoods such as mahogany were popular choices. Curved corner cupboards were common,

had libraries with built-in shelves. Originally, books were kept in closed cupboards, but as it became fashionable to display the spine bindings, solid oak or mahogany open shelving became commonplace. More ornate libraries featured glass-fronted built-in bookcases above closed cupboards. Ranks of drawers and

and dining rooms often featured a built-in sideboard, cut to fit into a recess in the wall. In libraries, bookshelves were usually sunk within a niche, their cornices flush with the wall surface.

Relatively little fitted furniture featured in houses during the Regency period through to the 1840s. Kitchens and servants' rooms retained their essential storage spaces, but as carpentry and joinery skills improved with the development of new tools, furniture was designed as free-standing units. American Federal and Empire houses featured shelved cupboards on fireplace walls in dining rooms and parlours to store china, silverware and books. Kitchen built-ins were of pine, often painted dark red and green.

Victorian England saw a burst of growth in fitted joinery. Built-in libraries and bedrooms in polished or painted hardwoods were promoted as the height of chic, and a 'cosy corner' seating area was often built into a corner or next to a fireplace. A kitchen dresser for storing china, initially with open shelves but later with glazed doors, was standard. American interiors followed a similar theme; window seats were popular in Shingle and Colonial Revival houses and in Arts and Crafts houses on both sides of the Atlantic.

Right Cut from a slab of solid granite, this sink is set into a built-in cupboard in the kitchen of Stephen Mack's home, Chase Hill Farm, in Rhode Island, USA. The cupboard, like the rest of the joinery in the kitchen, is decorated with Colonial-red milk paint. A selection of china is displayed on the open shelves above.

Above The built-in cupboards in the bathroom of the Burr Tavern, East Meredith, New York, were inspired by traditional Shaker designs. The encasement of sanitary units became increasingly fashionable in the 19th century.

Above The bathroom in the late 18th-century Chase Hill Farm contains a free-standing roll-top enamelled bathtub, with storage space provided by built-in pine cupboards, limed and treated with a translucent white stain.

Above A teak-topped open-front vanity unit in Christian Liaigre's house near La Rochelle, France. Provided it is regularly oiled, teak is highly resistant to moisture and is therefore well suited for use in bathrooms and kitchens.

In the early 20th century cupboards with solid doors and fine hinges and latches, glazed fitted cupboards for books and china, and peripheral seating areas in living or dining rooms were major elements in an Arts and Crafts house. Many architects experimented with fitted furniture. Charles Rennie Mackintosh's cupboards were often box-shaped and decorated with glass or metal inlay, mouldings, or paintwork, which echoed vertical wall motifs, and he often extended the fireplace area upwards and across to incorporate shelves. In America, Frank Lloyd Wright explored the sculptural options of built-in furniture, linking cupboards and seating areas to fireplaces and windows with repeating decorative motifs. Built-in dressing rooms became popular in the Edwardian era, as it was considered unhealthy to sleep in a room where clothes and shoes were stored. The years between the First and

Second World War also saw an increase in built-in furniture, largely as a space-saving measure. Modernists were in favour of as much furniture as possible being fitted, including cupboards, benches – often with hinged seats for storage – and built-in beds with shelves or drawers underneath, some houses even featured enclosed areas for a telephone, television and radio, the primary aim being to unify the rooms and leave living spaces uncluttered.

In the 1990s fitted furniture is taken for granted as the practicality of built-in cupboards has ensured their enduring popularity with an ever-increasing number of styles and finishes available. Built-in kitchens and bathrooms are masterpieces of fitted joinery, as are bedroom storage units. Yet in a living or dining space, fitted furniture is out of fashion – we have become a mobile population and like to take our furniture with us when we move on.

Left The white-painted plank-lined kitchen of Christian Liaigre's house near La Rochelle is furnished simply with bracketed natural-wood open shelving for storage and display, and built-under cupboards with tar-stained pine doors. These units are topped by a solid oiled teak work surface, into which is set a hob and a sink.

Left and below left The walls of the Kitchen House in this renovated 1920s island home in New Hampshire are lined with open shelving, on which crockery is stacked, and pine-slat units, from which an array of kitchenalia is hung on hooks made from wire coathangers.

Right The kitchen cupboards in the Burr Tavern are painted Prussian blue. This was a fashionable colour in the USA before the 1830s, but it is quite unusual to see it in its pure form, since the cost of the pigment meant it was often mixed with cheaper white paint, resulting in a lighter shade of blue.

Furniture

The heritage of furniture in a modern country interior can be traced back to the craft traditions of the early carpenters who first took a piece of timber and transformed it into a chair, a table or a simple cupboard. Whether fashioned in Scandinavia, in parts of Europe or America, or in the harsh climate of an Australian state, these early rustic pieces are connected to the present by an appreciation of the rugged and simple.

Making use of nature's bounty meant taking design cues from natural forms, and early furniture was extremely basic and purely functional: stools were simply collections of short, sturdy tree

Below left *The slatted base and seat of this rustic chair are made from kindling wood, and the back and the sides of the arms are cow hide.*

Below centre *A pair of Adirondacks-style armchair recliners flank a matching table on the deck of a house in Sun Valley, Idaho, USA.*

Bottom centre *Designed by architect Jim Ruscitto, this seat is carved into the top of a large standing-dead pine post that supports the outer edge of an open upstairs gallery in a log house in Aspen, Colorado, USA. The practice of carving a seat into the base of a tree trunk was well established in Scandinavia during the Middle Ages.*

Below right and bottom right *The deck furniture at a lodge near Aspen, is inspired by the twig-and-branch furniture of the Adirondacks. The wood for making the chairs was gathered from the forested slopes of the Rocky Mountains which lie beyond.*

Left On a porch in Aspen, east
comes to the west in the form of a
striking shield-back stick-and-
twig chair inspired by the rustic
furniture of the Adirondacks.

Below Rustic forked-branch stools
are among the earliest examples
of the woodsman's craft, and are
common in forested rural areas of
Europe, Scandinavia and the USA.

Bottom A pair of 'Bruyère' stools
in Christian Liaigre's house near
La Rochelle, France.

Left One of a number of wicker-work African chairs, in a modern post-and-beam house on Long Island, New York, USA.

Right The dining area in this restored 18th-century log farmhouse in Megève, France, is furnished with a stout plank-top table bought from a convent in Provence, and a set of sturdy but decorative carved-back Savoyard dining chairs.

Left One from a set of dining chairs designed by the American architect Mark Pynn. The seat, back and sides of the chair are made from slats of steamed and shaped wood, known as bentwood, secured onto a bentwood frame.

branches nailed to a round wooden top; likewise, a chair would have a smooth, flat seat, four legs and upright spindles for the back. Branches and twigs were bent and twisted into components for furniture, and country folk created solid chairs from stumps of trees, adding a simple cushion for comfort. Long pine tables have a tradition stretching back to the 16th century when they were used for eating, as a work surface and for holding meetings. An integral part of family and community life, the wooden table is still an essential addition to many modern kitchens.

Most furniture designs were evolved by the turner and the joiner, who developed the basic mortise-and-tenon method of joining pieces of wood together by slotting the projecting edge of one section into a matching recess cut into the other. Large pieces of primitive furniture, such as tables and cupboards, consisted of riven planks that had been hand-trimmed with a saw and adze and were held together with crudely made clout-headed nails. The joiner made chairs, bedsteads, tables, benches, cabinets, cupboards, linen presses, and anything that was panelled, dovetailed or pinned. The turner created pieces on a lathe, producing plain but useful stools, tables and everyday chairs. All kinds of wood, but especially oak, elm and pine, were fashioned into practical items, yet each piece yielded its individual beauty to the skill of the craftsman. A man who could sense the grain and form hidden beneath layers of moss and twigs was a man to value.

In Scandinavia, where winters are exceptionally long, men spent most of the time at woodworking, stretching their creativity to the limits and exploring and experimenting with the versatility of wood. Their high regard for combining beauty and function remains a strong part of their modern culture.

Almost without exception, Elizabethan furniture was massive in size, heavily panelled and intricately carved from oak. By the early 17th century, designs had become plainer, and the popular timbers were solid walnut, beech and ash woods, and fruitwood. The four-poster beds of this period were masterpieces of elegant carving and were hung with heavy cotton, linen and silk textiles. Provincial homes of the era had heavy oak panel-back chairs, with or without arms, with turned members and a rush seat.

In Europe, the USA and the Antipodes, the simple oak sideboard, the sturdy pine kitchen dresser and the beech ladder-back chair are icons of the 18th-century country cottage look. Another

Right and below right The influence of Japanese, Thai, Indonesian and Caribbean styles of architecture and design can be detected in the work of French designer Christian Liaigre. For example, in his furniture designs, he makes extensive use of durable, oily hardwoods, such as teak. He also closely relates the form of his furniture to its function. The result, as evident in the undraped four-poster bed and writing desk in his house near La Rochelle, is a pleasing simplicity of line that is reminiscent of Shaker style.

Below A simple plank-top frame table and four rustic rush-seated chairs furnish a plank-lined kitchen at Les Fermes de Marie, near Mont Blanc, in France.

Above Not so much a four-poster as a four-trunker – a simple twig and branch Adirondacks-style bed in a lodge near Aspen.

Above right A typical Savoyard wooden box bed in La Ferme d'Hauteluce, situated at the foot of Mont d'Arbois in France.

Right A Danish oak cupboard of c. 1620–30, which was probably originally built-in and intended for storing wool.

Right The simple Tibetan-blue painted panelling, introduced to this Dutch town house by its owner, the designer Ischa van Delft, provides an elegant backdrop for the 19th-century rush-seated country chairs.

Left The maple day bed and cherry-wood tallboy and four-poster bed in the Blue Chamber of the Silas Deane House in Wethersfield, Connecticut, USA, all date from the mid-18th century.

Left This bedroom in the Burr Tavern in East Meredith, New York, is furnished with a romantic four-poster bed from New England, dated c. 1810, hung with dimity fabric with a hand-woven French lace trim.

favourite piece of furniture in many wooden houses was the rocking chair, which dates from about 1760. The first design was a spindle-back chair with a pair of rockers that linked the front and back legs, similar to the rockers on cradles of the same period. By early Victorian times, the rocking chair had a flowing S-shaped back and seat, and the rockers were curved – bentwood (which was bent into shape with moulds after being heated with steam) first appeared in the mid-1880s. American rockers of this period had straight backs and were regarded as chairs for the elderly.

A classic Windsor chair made of ash sums up the style of the 18th century with its elegant presence. Popular in coffee houses because it withstood constant use without falling apart, the Windsor chair featured a saddle seat, round tapered mortise-and-tenon joints, legs that were not a continuation of the chair's back and arms – a design innovation – and the use of hooped wood in

With new, improved tools, skilful carpenters began to design and make more sophisticated, exquisitely crafted free-standing furniture.

the back, arms and stretchers. This combination made it different from any other chair of the period. A variation of the famous Windsor chair, known as the smoker's bow chair, was popular in 19th-century kitchens. It had the characteristic Windsor saddle seat and splayed, turned legs, but featured a low back and low, flat arms that were perfect for the pipe smoker to rest his elbow upon.

Although there have been subtle changes in construction, modern wooden furniture is derivative of the best of the design elements of the past and reflects traditions that were perfected over time. Many of the techniques that craftsmen of old persevered to perfect are revered by present-day furniture makers. Contemporary chairs, dining tables, occasional tables and storage trunks may be made of different types of wood, but the inspiration for their form nearly always comes from the past. The ingenuity of the early colonists has survived technological progress, and much of the modern wooden furniture that is still produced, either by hand or by small factories around the world, owes its

Below In this richly coloured house in New York State, built in c. 1835, a late 18th-century or early 19th-century comb-back rocker from the Boston area retains its original verdigris paint.

balance and integrity to shapes first seen centuries ago. The fabrics used for upholstery may be more hard wearing, and the wide choice of stain and paint finishes now available are longer lasting, but in the best furniture it is still the shape and grain of the wood that dictate the character of the end piece. Through the centuries a sense of scale has kept innovative designers true to form and use, as they mix old and new designs, combine rough textures with smooth, and incorporate decorations according to fashion.

Top In the Silas Deane House dining room are chairs from Rhode Island, USA, and a birdcage table from New York, both of mahogany, c. 1760.

Above The furniture in the Washington Bedroom of the Joseph Webb House in Wethersfield is late 18th century and typical American Chippendale.

Accessories

The sensuality of a wooden object is undeniable and its tactile quality is compelling: a carved walnut box, polished smooth from years of being handled; simple and functional Shaker boxes for hats, buttons, ribbons or sewing kit; photograph frames of rough bark; exquisitely carved mirror frames of fragrant wood; painted wooden eggs, originally created for the Easter ritual and now sought-after ornaments; and wooden tribal masks that will contain their magic forever. It is the texture of the timber as much as the form of the wooden object that is attractive both to look at and to touch. A walking stick of gnarled wood found on a country walk, or pieces of driftwood that can be twisted together with twine to make a unique base for a lampshade are perfect accessories for the

Below A collection of hand-painted Indian treenware sits on a glass-topped cane table in this home on Long Island, New York, USA.

Above In a log lodge near Aspen, Colorado, USA, pictures recalling the old West are mounted in twig-and-branch frames – one of which is displayed on a tepee-shaped stand.

interior of a wooden house. Nothing is pretentious or out of place, since the creation of each item has been inspired by the intrinsic quality of the wood as it has spoken to the craftsman.

Simple rustic items have been carved from wood for centuries: wooden spoons and ladles, broom handles, water pitchers, chopping boards, spinning wheels and other household necessities, as well as a plethora of toys that are now highly collectible. Scandinavian families, in particular, gathered inside during the cold winters and experimented with various woods and techniques to make balanced and beautiful utensils with designs refined through generations. Since the Industrial Revolution, numerous objects once crafted by hand have been mass-produced by machines, often using synthetic materials. The late 20th century has seen a rejection of the bland uniformity of these goods, causing a strong revival of interest in traditionally made wooden objects.

Below left This prototype coconut-wood lamp by Donghia Furniture/ Textiles sits on a table in this home on Long Island. Like many of the pieces produced by Donghia, the lamp base has a tactile sculptural quality.

Below right Consisting of small branches joined together at the top and interlaced with twigs, this lamp base, in a lodge in Aspen, looks organic rather than man-made.

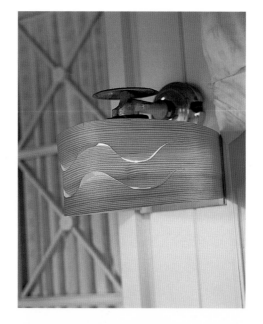

Left The wooden shade for this gas-powered wall lamp was made from cut veneer, steamed and curved into shape. Some of the earliest veneer shades were made in Sweden as long ago as the 17th century. The thin veneer allows light to shine through, highlighting the figuring and grain.

Right and far right In a log house, a craftsman is free to create ingenious objects from local materials. Here, an Adirondacks-inspired lamp stands on a massive side table hewn from a bark-off tree trunk. The small lamp stand is made from bark-on branches and the shade is a crudely cut veneer of silver birch bark.

165

Decorating Wood

Stepping from harsh sunlight into a softly lit room momentarily blinds one to the surroundings. It takes a minute to refocus, but then all becomes clearly visible: colours sharpen and patterns emerge from the shadows. Being in a painted wooden room is rather like that experience: it is impossible to see all of the details without stopping and focusing on one section of a colourful floor stencil, an intricate, regally gilded carving, or a naïvely painted frieze of frolicking mythical figures. The colourful, bold designs of folk art have been stamped on more pieces of furniture than can be counted and, when executed with skill, whether the imagery is romantic or in the heraldic tradition, it always reveals something about its history that can be

Home of Stephen Mack

interpreted by future generations. Walls alive with dancing shepherdesses, cupboards draped with garlands of

roses, a grandfather clock embellished with delicate flowers that appear to be growing across its surface;

alternatively, wall panels, floorboards and furniture that look marvellous with a simple paint or woodgrain

effect, or a natural oil, wax or varnish that highlights the grain – these are just some of the delights that

can be created from a plain piece of wood, transformed by the chosen finish in truly inspirational ways. The

following pages examine the most popular traditions for decorating wood and provide inspiration for

achieving some of the vast array of finishes – whether on floors, walls, or on individual pieces of furniture.

Colourwash, Paint and Decorative Finishes

Over the centuries a variety of washes and paints have been used to colour and protect the exterior and interior surfaces of wooden houses. For most of the 20th century, pre-mixed oil- and water-based paints have been favoured, available in an enormous range of colours. Early painters, however, had to mix their paints and washes on site, making do with locally available ingredients.

Limewash is the oldest of the traditional decorative finishes, first used in about 8000 BC. In its simplest form it is a milk-like

wash made by slaking lump lime in water to produce lime putty, which is then diluted with water and mixed with a waterproofing agent, such as linseed oil or animal fat. With several coats, it dries to an opaque white colour that is bright and luminous in sunlight, and mat or chalk-like when the weather is overcast. Coloured limewashes are produced by adding pigments – traditionally earth pigments, such as those derived from clay, or by-products of the mining industry, such as cobalt, cadmium, copper carbonate and iron oxide. Aside from its vibrancy of colour which mellows with age, limewash is semi-porous, so any moisture in the surface to which it is applied can evaporate, rather than remain trapped and cause decay. Moreover, the lime works as an anti-bacterial agent

Top left and right The rustic appearance of the overlapped split-weather-board walls of the cottage on the left contrasts with the more formal, urban look of the feathered-edge tongue-and-groove weatherboards at the rear of the Bellevue Homestead, Coominya, Australia. Both are painted in shades of red that are traditional to the region.

Above left and centre The Burr Tavern, built in East Meredith, New York, USA, in c. 1835, was originally painted white. Subsequently, the white-pine weatherboarding has been painted yellow ochre, and the doors and the window frames are Venetian red.

Above right Architect Tony Suttle's 'Queenslander' house near Brisbane, Australia, is clad with tongue-and-groove weatherboards, with a door hood covered in corrugated tin – both painted pale blue. Cream-coloured French windows open onto a veranda at the rear of the property.

Right The weatherboard exterior of Stephen Mack's 'Cape Cod' house, built in 1792 in Rhode Island, USA, is painted authentic Colonial red.

Below This Australian house features dark blue overlapped boards and an 'ironbark' roof.

Bottom To compensate for the power of the sun, Australian architect John Mainwaring employs strong colours on the subtropical houses he designs for Queensland's Sunshine Coast.

Left and far left
The visual contrast between these two houses is not only due to the exterior joinery, but also to the use of colour: contrasting shades highlight the details on the Australian house (far left); all white suppresses them on the New Zealand house (left).

and discourages insect infestation. These aesthetic and physical properties explain its widespread use until the late 19th century, mainly on cob or lime-rendered walls and on the wattle-and-daub infill panels of half-timbered houses, but also on external joinery.

Apart from the ubiquitous white, colours tended to reflect the pigmentation of local clays and mineral deposits from which most of the pigments were derived. In northern Europe, shades of

Right For the most part, the doors, chimneypiece, ladder-back chairs and 'Indian' shutters in the 18th-century Simon Huntington Tavern in Norwich, Connecticut, USA, retain their original milk paint finishes. These were discovered under layers of subsequently applied paint during Stephen Mack's restoration. Where the original paint had deteriorated or was missing, modern milk paints in authentic period colours were applied.

Below Along with the rest of the interior, the stairway hall of the late 18th-century Joseph Webb House in Wethersfield, Connecticut, was repainted with oil paints colour-matched to the original Georgian green and lilac.

Below centre This hall in the Issac Stevens house, built in 1778–9 in Wethersfield, features fielded panelling and a turned balustrade painted in 18th-century beige drab.

cream, buff, mustard, pale brown and green, dusty pink and red were most in evidence, while in southern Europe, darker, more vibrant colours, such as mauve-blue and acid yellow, were found. In Scandinavia, where most wooden exteriors were left unpainted until around the mid-19th century, colours as diverse as creamy ochre, pale yellow, tawny orange, pale and purplish blues, salmon pink and rust red were fashionable, while in the USA, intense, mat, earthy colours, such as red-brown, terracotta and marigold have been used since the Colonial period.

Above right Planked walls in an early 18th-century Norwegian kitchen, were repainted in traditional cobalt blue.

Right The hallway of this house, built in Norway at the turn of the 17th century, features chamfered-plank walls, and a door and architrave painted in authentic period pink and dark green.

Right White-painted plank walls and other joinery in the Bedroom House, an annexe of an early 20th-century house built on an island in New Hampshire, USA. The owners chose white for a Caribbean feel and to cool the interior during the hot, humid summers.

Far right Pale-blue planked walls provide a cool backdrop to a variety of stained and polished woods in The Battery in Kent, England – built as a sailors' billet and later used as a holiday home for disadvantaged children.

Below Prussian blue was a highly fashionable colour during the early 19th century. In the Burr Tavern it is used on the stiles of the doors where it contrasts with red oxide moulding and yellow ochre panels.

Prior to the mid-19th century, lime-wash was also applied to internal walls and joinery. However, it tended to rub off when brushed against, and so was supplanted by whitewash, a simple mixture of whiting (ground, washed chalk) and animal glue, dissolved in water and coloured, if desired, with powder pigments. Whitewash dries to give an opaque finish and exhibits a range and an intensity of tones similar to limewash. Yet although it is very effective on plastered walls, it is not especially durable when used on timber, and

will soon flake off if the underlying wood has too high a moisture content. Consequently, painters tended to use more resilient media, especially for exposed external wood, such as weatherboards.

Below A Prussian blue architrave frames a woodgrained door in the Burr Tavern. The simulation of the wood's heart grain is by artist Doug Vickers, who used Williamsburg pink-brown over a stone and yellow ochre ground.

Above left and right At Stephen Mack's home, Chase Hill Farm, the traditional character of the interior has been retained with flaking whitewash covering the walls, and blue milk paint on the doors.

For wealthier clients, decorators would mix oil-based paints by grinding earth and mineral pigments into powder, mixing them with whiting to lighten the colour, and blending them into boiled linseed oil and turpentine. Although durable, these forerunners of the pre-mixed oil-based paints of the 20th century, were time-consuming to make and apply (in two or three coats), and were thus expensive. Casein paint, however, was easier both to make and apply, and was almost as durable as oil-based paint. Also known as milk paint, it is made by colouring buttermilk or skimmed milk with vegetable or earth pigments usually derived

Opposite left and right This full-height pine chimney wall of raised panelling has been meticulously scraped down to its original blue-green milk paint by the restorer Stephen Mack. In areas where the scraping broke through to the wood, a wash of milk paint was mixed and applied.

Right and below The wall panelling and panelled doors in this elegant drawing room in a late 17th-century house in Spitalfields, London, England, are painted a dark royal blue and then gilded. The owner has used silver Dutch metal leaf on the large panels, and gold metal leaf on the quadrant mouldings that surround them. The gilded surfaces were then antiqued with wire wool in order to create an air of faded opulence that is perfectly in character with the furniture, soft furnishings and rugs in the room.

from local plants or clay. To inhibit fungal growth or insect infestation a little lime was usually added to the mix. Applied in one or two quick-drying coats, it produced an opaque finish with a subtle mat-satin sheen. Milk paint was used on exterior and interior woodwork and furniture in Europe and Scandinavia from the 17th century onwards, and also in the Antipodes during the 19th and early 20th centuries. Yet it is most commonly associated with 18th-century American Colonial and late 19th- and early 20th-century Colonial Revival houses, in which the plank walls, panels,

window frames, staircases and doors were almost exclusively decorated with this finish. Favourite colours included white, mustard, sage and dark green, gray-mauve, berry and rust red, and black.

Gilding was a popular form of decoration for wooden surfaces, especially panelling and moulding. The technique involves sticking thin sheets of gold leaf or gold powder onto wooden or plaster surfaces, and then burnishing them to a shiny, lustrous finish. Traditionally, a thin layer of red clay (bole), or red-painted gesso was applied under the leaf or powder to impart a warm glow to the gilding. Since the Middle Ages, gilding has been employed as a show of opulence in many grand houses, applied to the flutes of columns, wooden carvings, wooden and plaster mouldings, furniture, mirror frames and numerous artefacts.

In addition to gilding, a variety of specialist techniques can be used to decorate wood with colour, patterns and motifs, that were derived from itinerant artists who travelled the land decorating interiors and artefacts for money, bed or board. The most popular were stencilling, folk art, woodgraining and marbling.

Below far left This cupboard in the Sønstebø Farmhouse in Heddal, Norway, was decorated in the 1840s by father and son painters, Olav and Olav Langerud. The use of bright colours was integral to folk art in most of Scandinavia where the hours of daylight were few during the winter months, and the blue and terracotta colours are typical of the region.

Below left The stiles and rails of this farmhouse door are golden-oak grained, and the centre panels are painted in Scandinavian-Baroque and Chinese style. The decoration was signed by Hallvor Dalane in 1864.

Below and below right The floral motifs on the beds at Sønstebø were inspired by flowers that the painters had picked in the locality and dried.

Stencilling involves transferring patterns and motifs onto a surface by applying paints or dyes through cut-outs in a stencil made from materials as diverse as wood, bone, leather, leaves, oiled cardboard and, nowadays, acetate. Before the introduction of hand-painted wallpapers at the end of the 17th century, repeating stencilled motifs were used throughout Europe to decorate wall hangings and walls. Thereafter, although stencilled friezes and dados incorporating Classical or floral motifs featured in many 19th-century urban interiors, from the 18th century the practice was largely confined to rural areas where wallpapers were either unavailable, expensive, or unsuitable for wood or plaster surfaces subject to damp. Stencilling was also applied to joinery, furniture, floors and floorcloths, the patterns mainly inspired by rural imagery, with animals, birds, fruit, flowers and leaves the recurring subjects. The similarity between designs found in Scandinavia, Europe and North America is explained by the fact that most artists working in America were of German, Dutch, Swiss, Swedish and Norwegian origins. Parallels were further consolidated in the late 19th century by the production of pre-cut 'pattern-box' stencils, which meant artists no longer had to cut their own designs.

Above At Brookgate, an English timber-framed house dating from 1350 (with later additions in 1500 and 1612), the plaster infill panels are coated with limewash, traces of which can also be seen on the exposed beams.

Freedom of artistic expression remained unfettered in the hand-painted folk art that embellished many rural European, Scandinavian and North American wooden houses from the Middle Ages to the early 20th century. Like stencilled decoration, folk art was primarily inspired by rural imagery, with the most exuberant examples found on furniture and interior joinery in southern Germany, Alpine regions, Sweden and Norway. The most sophisticated work appears in Scandinavian countries, where log or wood-lined walls were often decorated with large pictorial murals depicting historical, religious or rustic scenes. In Norway, a form of folk art known as rose painting (from the Norwegian word *rosemaling*, which literally means decorative painting) developed and reached its height of popularity between 1800 and 1850. Although large roses and other floral garlands were often a feature, rose painting broadly covered many secular and religious subjects, with styles varying from valley to valley.

Developed by the ancient Egyptians, woodgraining is a means of simulating the appearance of wood with paints and glazes. In regions where there was an abundance of relatively cheap, fast-growing softwoods, there was little need to practice woodgraining. However, slow-growing, expensive hardwoods – prized for their distinctive figuring and grain – have been in increasingly short

Opposite far left The bedroom in this Norwegian farmhouse was painted in 1922 by Knut Hovden, a teacher of decorative rose painting (rosemaling) at a time when this style of folk art was enjoying a revival.

Left and opposite right Also by Knut Hovden in the same farmhouse, the rose painting is based on traditional styles, but is less free-flowing and employs brighter colours than examples from previous centuries.

Right and far right The ground floor of the Ramberg Farmhouse at the Bygdetunet Museum in Heddal was constructed during the early 18th century. Originally, furniture and joinery in the room was covered with rose painting. However, during the second half of the 19th century this traditional form of Scandinavian decoration was sometimes covered with woodgraining. The golden-oak graining applied here became highly fashionable around 1880.

A variety of paints, colourwashes and varnishes could be applied in a range of decorative techniques to alter the appearance of wood.

Above The first floor of the Ramberg Farmhouse was added in 1780, and the guest room shown here was decorated by Olav Hansson with biblical scenes, inscriptions and rose painting in 1784.

Right The Fyrileiv-Stugo Farmhouse in Oslo, Norway, was built in 1930. The traditional painted decorations on the doors, cornice and brush-stand are executed in a more formal Baroque style than those at Ramberg.

Above Painted in traditional blue, yellow and clay brown, the biblical scenes and floral motifs in the main bedroom at Ramberg incorporate an inscription that says the 'house is protected against thieves and fire'.

supply since the late 17th century. Apart from using veneers, the solution was to make furniture and architectural fixtures from softwood, and grain them to imitate hardwoods, such as oak, walnut, mahogany, chestnut, rosewood, maple and satinwood. Woodgraining was either sophisticated and hard to distinguish from real wood, or a stylized theatrical illusion, with the figuring and grain crudely suggested. The latter, often referred to as folk graining, is more closely associated with the interiors of rural houses, the former with grander urban interiors.

Simulating the appearance of marble and other stones with paint and glazes was first practised by the ancient Greeks and Romans. Like woodgraining, it is still used in areas where the genuine material is unavailable or too expensive. Realistic faux marbled panels, pillars, floors, fireplaces, moulding and furniture featured in grand urban and rural houses, especially where the decor was inspired by Classicism. However, naïve examples can be found in many smaller rural houses, particularly in Sweden and Norway. This 'rustic', or 'farmer', marbling is characterized by fantasy patterns and opaque, often gaudy colouring that bear little resemblance to the intricate veining, subtle translucency and depth of colour of the more sophisticated urban equivalents.

Natural Finishes

Various stains, varnishes, oils, waxes and pastes can be applied to wood to enhance or alter its natural colouring without masking the figuring and grain. Chemical stains react with the tannic acid in wood to produce subtle colour changes – ammonia gives mahogany a dark-brown hue with a grey cast. Water-based stains, made of earth-coloured pigments dissolved in water, produce vivid colours and are best applied to close-grained softwoods. Spirit-based stains, where the pigment is dissolved in methylated spirits and shellac, result in duller colouring and are most effective on oily hardwoods. Oil-based stains, consisting of oil pigments, naphtha and white spirit, produce the most consistent coloration and are used on fine hardwoods.

To protect and enrich stained or unstained wood, translucent or opaque 'microporous' finishes are increasingly favoured for external and internal joinery, but traditional spirit- and oil-based varnishes are still used. On open-grained hardwoods, such as oak and teak, boiled or raw linseed oil, which darkens the wood and produces a soft surface sheen, is applied instead of varnish. Wax polish is preferred on furniture made from close-grained hardwoods, such as walnut and mahogany. Sometimes tinted with pigments, traditional polish consists of pure beeswax, carnuba wax and methylated spirits, and repeated applications and buffing create a lustrous patina.

Right A pine door, staircase and limed floor in a post-and-beam weatherboard house built during the 1980s in the largest pinewood forest in New York State, USA.

To bleach the colour of wood and create a grey-white chalky appearance, liming pastes and waxes are used, which protect the wood. Hardwearing pastes are usually applied to floors and panelling, while less durable waxes are mostly used on furniture. On open-grained woods the white pigment is deposited in the grain and highlights it in relation to the surrounding surface; on close-grained woods a more even, opaque finish is produced.

Below The squared-log walls and planked doors in this combined bedroom and bathroom in a restored 18th-century farmhouse in Megève, France, have been limed and then given additional protection with an application of clear varnish. The log farmhouse was originally located in the Grand-Bornand region, and was transported to its present site by its owner, the interior designer Michèle Rédélé.

Bottom left and right The Hotel Mont-Blanc in Megève was renovated in 1949 by Georges Boisson. The walls of the comfortable bedrooms still retain their original 19th-century pine panelling and pocket doors, which are designed to slide into recesses in the wall. The natural finish of the golden wood creates a feeling of warmth and enhances the attractive markings and grain.

Top This stunning 17th-century stained and waxed hardwood wall panelling was introduced to a restored 16th-century timber-framed manor house in England.

Above This custom-made, unobtrusive teak grill for heating and air-conditioning was finished to match the antique pine floorboards in a barn, designed and restored by Stephen Mack.

Carving and Turning

Decorative carving and elegant turning has featured prominently in wooden houses around the world. Both are skilled and time-consuming crafts, so their extent and sophistication has tended to reflect status and affluence. Exteriors and interiors alike display a vast array of geometric patterns, strapwork, arabesques, heraldic and Classical motifs, and stylized or naturalistic animals and foliage on doors, posts, architraves, brackets, beams, panels and stairs.

Below left The decorative fretwork, in the shape of hearts and flowers, carved scrolls and ovolo and cyma reversa mouldings, displays a fine attention to authentic exterior detail on this 'Swiss chalet', built in 1950 in Sun Valley, Idaho, USA.

Below right The Alpine-style decoration of the chalet is enhanced by painted edelweiss, the small flowering plant native to the European Alps and a recurring motif in vernacular Swiss architecture.

Bottom right Dragon House in Smarden, Kent, England, is a traditional medieval half-timbered house, which had the elaborately decorated dragon frieze added to it in the 17th century.

Top left and right *The Green Parlour at Athelhampton House, Dorset, England, a historically important 15th-century house, was designed by Alfred Cart de Lafontaine in c. 1880. The room takes its name from the green silk wall panels, which are divided by Corinthian oak pilasters. Equally striking is the Tudor-style linenfold panelling on the window shutters. Delicately carved in oak, the panelling is employed extensively throughout the house.*

Above left *The Silas Deane House, built in 1766 in Wethersfield, Connecticut, USA, features an open-string staircase with elaborate mahogany balusters.*

Above right *A Georgian open-string staircase with a square newel post and turned balustrade in an 18th-century house in Stonington, Connecticut, restored by Stephen Mack.*

Directory

Helpful Organizations

The following trade and professional organizations offer information, guidelines and technical support; write for more information.

British Decorators Association
32 Coton Road
Nuneaton
Warwickshire CV11 5TW
England

British Wood Preserving Association
Building No 6
The Office Village
4 Romford Road
London E15 4EA
England

Building Conservation Trust
Apartment 39
Hampton Court Palace
East Molesey
Surrey KT8 9BS
England

The Guild of Master Craftsmen
Castle Place
166 High Street
Lewes
East Sussex BN7 1XU
England

The International Council on Monuments and Sites
UK Wood Committee
10 Barley Mow Passage
London W4 4PH
England

Royal Incorporation of Architects in Scotland
15 Rutland Square
Edinburgh EH1 2BE
Scotland

Royal Institute of British Architects
66 Portland Place
London W1N 4AD
England

Society for the Protection of Ancient Buildings
37 Spital Square
London E1 6DY
England

Architects, Interior Designers & Builders

Acanthus Associated Architectural Practices Ltd
Voysey House
Barley Mow Passage
London W4 4PN
England

Architype (Architects)
4–6 The Hop Exchange
24 Southwark Street
London SE1 1TY
England

Carnachan Architects Ltd
(Architects, interior designers and landscape architects)
27 Bath Street
Parnell
PO Box 37-717
Auckland
New Zealand

Conger Fuller Architects
710 East Durant Street
Aspen
CO 81611
USA

Cowper, Griffith & Brimblecombe
(Architects)
The Barn
College Farm
Whittlesford
Cambridge CB2 4LX
England

Donghia UK Ltd Showroom
(Interior, textile and furniture designers)
23 The Design Centre
Chelsea Harbour
London SW10 0XE
England

Victor Farrer Partnership
(Architects)
57 St Peter's Street
Bedford
Bedfordshire MK40 2PR
England

Dave Fritchley
(Log detailing/twig work and rustic furniture specialist)
Eggshole Cottage
Starvecrow Lane
Peasmarsh
East Sussex TN3 16XN
England

Roderick James and Co
(Architects)
Seagull House
Dittisham Mill Creek
Dartmouth
Devon TQ6 0HZ
England

Kenström Design Pty Ltd
(Architects)
92 Cathedral Street
Woolloomooloo
NSW 2011
Australia

Christian Liaigre
(Furniture and interior designer)
Bureau d'Études
122 rue de Grenelle
75007 Paris
France

Holly Lueders Design
(Building, interior and furniture design)
27 West 67 Street
New York
NY 10023
USA

Rob and Sarah McConnell
(Builder and paint specialist)
8 Coastguard Cottages
Coastguard Square
Rye Harbour
East Sussex TN31 7TS
England

McCurdy & Co Ltd
(Architects)
Manor Farm
Stanford Dingley
Reading
Berkshire RG7 6LS
England

Darryl Charles McMillen
(Architects)
PO Box 1068
Sun Valley
ID 83353
USA

Stephen P Mack Associates
(Architectural design and supplier of 18th-century houses and barns)
Chase Hill Farm
Ashaway
RI 02804
USA

John Mainwaring & Associates Pty Ltd
(Architects and urban designers)
PO Box 958
Noosa Heads
Queensland 4567
Australia

Jean-Jacques Massé
(Antique dealer)
Lange Strikstraat 14
5301 EE Zaltbommel
Holland

Moss Co Architects
Brookgate
Plealey
Shrewsbury SY5 0UY
England

Michèle Rédélé
(Interior designer)
90 Boulevard Malegerbes
Paris 75008
France

Ruscitto, Latham, Blanton
(Architects)
PO Box 419
Sun Valley
ID 83353
USA

September
(Interior decoration)
Vughterstraat 72
5211 GK's-Hertogenbosch
Holland

Shope, Reno, Wharton Associates
(Architects)
18 West Putnam Avenue
Greenwich
CT 06830
USA

Sunnit Architects
10 Attunga Lane
Mount Glorious
Queensland 4520
Australia

Olivier Vidal and Associates
(Architects)
14 rue Moncey
75009 Paris
France

Woods Bagot Pty Ltd Architects
64 Marine Parade
Southport
Queensland 4215
Australia

Materials Suppliers

Architectural Heritage Ltd
Taddington Manor
Taddington
Nr Cheltenham
Gloustershire GL54 5RY
England

Carvers and Gilders
9 Charterhouse Works
Eltringham Street
London SW18 1TD
England

Crowther of Syon Lodge
Busch Corner
London Road
Isleworth
Middlesex TW7 5BH
England

**The Great Northern Architectural
Antiques Co Ltd**
New Russia Hall
Chester Road
Tattenhall
Cheshire CH3 9AH
England

The House Hospital
68 Battersea High Street
London SW11 3HX
England

**The London Architectural Salvage
& Supply Co Ltd**
St Michael's Church
Mark Street
London EC2A 4ER
England

Mounts Hill Woodcraft Ltd
Turnden Road
Cranbrook
Kent TN17 2QL
England

Stuart Interiors
Barrington Court
Barrington
Nr Ilminster
Somerset TA19 0NQ
England

Walcot Reclamation
108 Walcot Street
Bath
Avon BA1 5BG
England

**Wansdown Joinery Works
(Southern) Ltd**
327 Lillie Road
London SW6 7NR
England

Paint, Wash and Varnish Suppliers

Lawrence T Bridgeman
No 1 Church Road
Roberttown
West Yorkshire WF15 7LS
England

H J Chard and Son
Albert Road
Bristol BS2 0XS
England

Cole & Son Ltd
142–144 Offord Road
London N1 1NS
England

Farrow & Ball Ltd
33 Uddens Trading Estate
Wimborne
Dorset BH21 7NL
England

Fired Earth PLC
Twyford Mill
Oxford Road
Adderbury
Oxfordshire OX17 3HP
England

Heart of the Country Centre
Swinfen
Nr Litchfield
Staffordshire WS14 9QR
England

Historic Paints Ltd
Burr Tavern
Route 1, PO Box 474
East Meredith
NY 13757
USA

Liberon Waxes Ltd
Mountfield Industrial Estate
Learoyd Road
New Romney
Kent TN28 8XU
England

Paint Library
5 Elystan Street
Chelsea Green
London SW3 3NT
England

Papers & Paints Ltd
4 Park Walk
London SW10 0AD
England

Potmolen Paints
27 Woodcock Industrial Estate
Warminster
Wiltshire BA12 9DX
England

Museums, Houses and Hotels of Interest

Athelhampton House
Athelhampton
Dorchester
Dorset DT2 7LG
England

Bellevue Homestead
Opposite Coominya Hotel
Coominya
Queensland 4311
Australia

The Buttolph Williams House
249 Broad Street
Wethersfield
CT 06109
USA

Glomdalsmuseet
Museum for Østerdalen and Solor
2400 Elverum
Norway

Heddal-og Nottodden Museum
Bygdetunet
Heddal
Norway

The Hempstead House
11 Hempstead Street
New London
CT 06320
USA

**The Historical Museum
of Telemark**
Ovregt 41
3715 Skien
Norway

Hotel Mont-Blanc
Place de l'Église;
Les Fermes de Marie
Chemin de Riante Colline;
Les Fermes des Grand Champ
Choseaux
74120 Megève
France

Mayes Cottage
36 Mawarra Street
Kingston
Queenland 4114
Australia

**Museum of Lakeland Life
& Industry**
Abbot Hall
Kendal
Cumbria LA9 6BT
England

Museum of Welsh Life
St Fagan's
Cardiff CF5 6XB
Wales

The Norwegian Folk Museum
Museumsvn 10 Bygdøy
Oslo
Norway

Roseland Cottage
204 Roseland Parkroad
Woodstock
CT 06281
USA

Ellen Terry Museum
Smallhythe Place
Smallhythe
Nr Tenterden
Kent TN30 7NG
England

The Webb-Deane-Stevens Museum
211 Main Street
Wethersfield
CT 06109
USA

Glossary

A

Acanthus: A popular decorative motif used in Classical and Gothic architecture, based on the leaves of a Mediterranean plant.

Adam style: Architecture, interiors and furniture in the Neoclassical style pioneered by the English brothers Robert (1728–92) and James Adam (1732–94) during the late 18th century.

Adobe: Sun-dried – as opposed to baked – brick.

Aesthetic movement: A late 19th-century English and American movement formed as a reaction to 'Philistine' high Victorian clutter in architecture and interior design. A precursor to Art Nouveau, it reflected a strong Japanese influence and overlapped with the Arts and Crafts movement.

Arabesques: A sculpted or painted ornament consisting of intertwined foliage and other forms.

Architrave: The moulded framework surrounding a door, window or arch.

Art Nouveau: A style of decoration and design that had its roots in the Arts and Crafts movement. Characterized by curves and flowing lines, asymmetry, and flower and leaf motifs, it was prevalent from the 1880s to 1914, particularly in mainland Europe.

Arts and Crafts movement: A movement initiated primarily by William Morris (1834–96) in Britain during the 1860s, and influential on both sides of the Atlantic until the mid-1920s. A reaction to the poor quality of many mass-produced goods following the Industrial Revolution, it advocated a return to traditional methods of craftsmanship to restore the integrity of architecture and design.

B

Balloon framing: A method of timber-frame construction, invented in Chicago in the 1830s and prevalent throughout the USA. It features vertical wall studs that extend from sill to eaves, to which the horizontal timbers and boards of the house are nailed.

Baluster: A short, vertical post, usually turned but sometimes carved. Also known as a banister.

Balustrade: A series of balusters supporting a rail or coping.

Bargeboard: A wide, flat board used to seal the space below the roof and the wall on a gable end. Often embellished with carved or pierced decoration. Also known as a vergeboard.

Baroque: An ornate style associated with 17th-century Italian architecture. It is characterized by the use of Classical proportions and motifs, such as cupids and cornucopias set in symmetrical, curvaceous designs.

Beaux-Arts style: A strand of late 19th-century Classicism based on the teachings of the influential École des Beaux-Arts in Paris, France, which were inspired by the architecture of Roman antiquity. Many American students attended the college after 1846, and consequently Beaux-Arts style had a major influence on American architecture during the second half of the 19th century.

Boss: An ornamental knob or projection covering the intersection of ribs in a vault or ceiling.

Box framing (see illustration): A traditional method of timber-frame construction, in which buildings are made up of a series of square or rectangular boxes (bays), each consisting of four timber-framed walls, made up of vertical and horizontal members, usually mortise-and-tenoned together. The end walls (the gable panels) had a roof gable structure attached to the top of them and most of the weight of the roof was borne by the corner posts of the bays. To accommodate a doorway or window, horizontal members would be left out and diagonal braces inserted to reinforce the wall.

C

Capital: The head or top of a column or pilaster.

Casement window: A window frame hinged on one side so that it swings out or in to open.

Chamfer: The surface created by cutting off the corner of a square or rectangular block of wood or stone, usually at an angle of 45 degrees.

Chinking: A mortar-like mix laid between horizontal wall logs. Very early chinking mixtures consisted of hay or pine twigs and clay. Cement-based versions were in widespread use during the 19th century. In recent times, acrylic latex versions have gained in popularity, owing to their greater flexibility and insulative properties.

Classicism: Revivals of the principles and forms of ancient Greek and Roman architecture. There have been numerous revivals and reinterpretations since the Italian Renaissance of the 15th and 16th centuries, when printed illustrated treatises, engravings and pattern books of the monuments and ruins of the Roman Empire first become widely available. During the 18th century they were augmented by increasing knowledge of ancient Greek and Roman architecture as a result of excavations at Pompeii and Herculaneum. This resulted in the Neoclassicism of Adam style, Empire style, Federal style and the Greek Revival (of the late 18th and early 19th century). Late 19th- and early 20th-century Classicism resulted in the Queen Anne Revival, Italianate style and Baroque Revival. In the 20th century, much of Modernist architecture was loosely based on Classical forms.

Closed string: A staircase in which the profile of treads and risers is covered at the side by a sloping member which supports the balustrade.

Cob: An ancient building material, primarily British, of clay mixed with chopped straw.

Coffered ceiling: A ceiling in which the beams and cross beams leave a regular pattern of square or multi-sided sunken panels (coffers), which can be embellished with moulding, carved, or painted.

Colonial style: The styles of architecture prevalent in North American colonies during the 17th and 18th centuries. During the 17th century, the late medieval style dominated American architecture, and during the 18th century Georgian Classicism came to the fore.

Colonial Revival: Late 19th- and early 20th-century styles of American architecture, sometimes referred to as neo-Georgian and ranging from replications of Georgian and American Colonial houses to a looser interpretation of Classical-style buildings as in the Queen Anne Revival, Stick and Shingle styles of the 1880s and 1890s.

Corbel: A projecting timber or stone block, often carved, supporting a horizontal member.

Corinthian: One of the most ornate of the Classical Orders of architecture, in which columns are slender and usually fluted, their capitals elaborately carved with acanthus leaves.

Timber-frame Construction

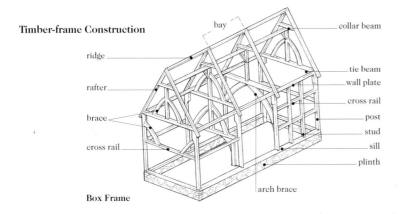

Box Frame

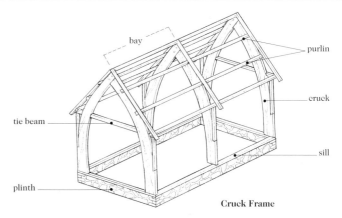

Cruck Frame

Corner notching and log-end profiles (see illustration): In traditional log-house construction, the horizontal wall logs are cut or notched to intersect alternately with one another at the corners of the building. The ends of the logs can then be cut and shaped to various decorative profiles. Among the many examples are: **A** Plumb log ends, **B** Beaver-cut log ends, **C** Staggered log ends, **D** Arched log ends.

Cornice: A projecting moulding located where the ceiling or roof meets the wall. In Classical architecture it is the projecting top of an entablature – the top of an Order, made up of an architrave, frieze and cornice.

Craftsman movement: An architectural and design movement that emerged from the Arts and Crafts movement in the USA during the first two decades of the 20th century. Promoted by Gustav Stickley (1847–1942) through his publication *The Craftsman* (1901–16), it advocated a holistic approach to living in which the house worked as a harmonious unit. It is best seen in the spacious Californian houses built by Charles Sumner Greene (1868–1957) and his brother Henry (1870–1954), who combined beautiful woods with the highest-quality joinery work.

Crown glass: An early form of window glass, cut from blown glass discs.

Cruck framing (see illustration): A method of timber framing in which pairs of crucks, or blades, usually curved timbers, extend either from the ground or low side-walls to the ridge of the roof. The crucks are the chief load-bearing members that support the weight of the roof.

D

Dado: The lower section of a wall surface, extending from about waist height down to the top of the skirting board, often defined by a dado rail, or chair rail – a moulding fixed to the wall to prevent the backs of chairs from damaging the surface.

Dog-leg stair: Two flights running parallel to each other, with a half-landing in between.

Doric: The earliest and plainest of the Classical Orders – each of which has its own distinctive proportions and detailing – in which columns usually have no base, a thick and broadly fluted shaft, and an unornamented capital.

Dormer: A roof projection set into the slope of a roof, usually containing a window.

Dragon style: Also known as Viking style; a style of architecture popular in Sweden, Denmark and Norway in the 19th century. A mixture of traditional log and timber-frame construction, the style is an expression of pride in the Viking Age, characterized by Dragon figureheads, other seafaring motifs and ornamental fretwork.

E

Eastlake style: A style of architecture, but more particularly interior design and furniture, based on the writings of Charles Locke Eastlake (1833–1906), notably *Hints on Household Taste in Furniture, Upholstery and other Details*. Stylistically, Eastlake provided a significant link between Gothic Revival and the early Arts and Crafts movement. The essence of the style lay in a rejection of the extravagances of Rococo and a promulgation of Jacobean, medieval German and early English designs. Characteristics included details such as turned baluster finials and knobs, and geometric applied ornament, often incised in thin bands, on mouldings and pilasters.

Egg-and-dart moulding: A decorative moulding carved with alternating ovals and arrowheads.

Empire style: An early 19th-century Neoclassical style in French interior decoration and furniture that reflected Napoleon Bonaparte's military and cultural endeavours. Characteristics included numerous Classical and Egyptian motifs. The style was prevalent in America in c. 1810–30.

English bond: Brickwork where courses of header bricks alternate with courses of stretcher bricks.

Etruscan style: Interior decoration, furniture and ceramics inspired by the arts and crafts of the ancient civilization of Etruria, centred in Tuscany and part of Umbria in Italy, from the 7th century BC until c. 200 BC. Characterized by the use of red, black and white, and motifs such as lions, birds, sphinxes, harpies and griffins.

F

Federal style: The predominant style of architecture and design in America between 1776, following the Declaration of Independence, and c. 1830. Based on English Adam style,

notable characteristics include arched windows, fanlights and delicate columns on exteriors, and interiors richly decorated with festoons, rosettes, urns and scrolling foliage, and the symbol of the Federal Union, the American eagle.

Field: The upper part of a wall, extending from the frieze or cornice down to the dado.

Finial: An ornament on top of a spire, pinnacle, gable, post, etc.

Flemish bond: A method of bricklaying in which alternate headers and stretchers are used in each course of bricks on the face of a wall.

Fluting: Shallow vertical grooves cut or carved into the surface of a column or post.

French windows: A pair of casement windows that reach to the floor and are hinged on the outer edges to swing open in the middle.

Fretwork: A band of horizontal and vertical lines forming a geometrical pattern.

Frieze: The middle section of an entablature; a panel below the cornice of a wall.

G

Gable: The part of a wall located immediately under the end of a pitched roof, cut into a triangular shape by the sloping sides of the roof.

Georgian: Styles of architecture and design during the reigns of George I (1714–27), George II (1727–60) and George III (1760–1820) of England. The style of the early period was Palladian – a restrained form of Classicism. Rococo, Gothic and Chinoiserie elements came to the fore from the 1830s to the mid-18th century, after which Neoclassicism became fashionable via Adam style in England and Federal style in America, with Gothic, Egyptian, Chinoiserie and Greek Revival elements.

Gesso: Plaster of Paris, applied to wood as a ground for painting and gilding.

Gothic: The predominant style of architecture during the Middle Ages, characterized by pointed arches, ribbed vaults, flying buttresses, arcading, galleries, window tracery, and naturalistic ornamentation on spandrels, canopies, niches and porches.

Gothic Revival: A late 18th- and 19th-century revival of Gothic architecture and ornamentation.

Greek Revival: A strand of Neoclassicism inspired by the buildings of ancient Greece, which dominated European and, later, American architecture and design from the 1750s to 1850s.

Grotesques: Carved or painted decorations, consisting of bizarre or fanciful depictions of animal, human and plant forms.

H

Half-timbering: A construction method in which vertical and horizontal timbers make up the frame of a wall, which is then filled in with lath and plaster, wattle and daub, stone or brick.

Hardwood: Dense, durable timber cut from slow-growing deciduous trees. Notable examples include oak, mahogany and walnut.

Log-wall Profiles

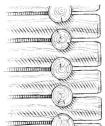

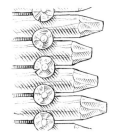

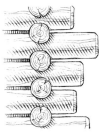

A Plumb log ends   B Beaver-cut log ends   C Staggered log ends   D Arched log ends

Herringbone: A decorative pattern in the shape of the spine of a herring. When used as a pattern for brickwork, the bricks slope in different directions in alternate rows.

Hood: A projecting moulding above a door or window designed to protect it from the rain.

I

Ionic: One of the Classical Orders, characterized by fluted columns and prominent volutes on the capitals – the top of a column or pilaster.

Italian Renaissance: The classicizing of Italian architecture during the 15th and 16th centuries.

Italianate: Mid-19th-century style of architecture in England and America, based on the rural architecture of Northern Italy and Italian Renaissance palaces, characterized by low roofs, overhanging eaves with decorative brackets, entrance towers, round-headed windows with hood mouldings, corner quoins, arcaded porches and balustraded balconies.

J

Jacobean: Historical period embracing the reigns of James I and Charles I of England (1603–49). The architecture was initially a mixture of late Tudor with Dutch gables and ornate chimneys, but evolved to more classical and symmetrical schemes based on Renaissance precedents. Characteristics included strapwork, obelisks, balustrades, niches and elaborately moulded panels. Oak furniture and wooden panelling was richly carved, and there was an extensive use of heraldic, military and emblematic motifs.

Jetty: An overhanging upper storey.

Joists: Horizontal timbers laid parallel to provide a support for floorboards.

L

Lath: A thin slip of wood.

Leaded lights: Small panes of glass set into lead strips (cames) to form a window.

Lights: Generally, panes of glass, but also the opening between mullions.

Linenfold panelling: Wooden panelling in which the individual panels are carved to look like the vertical folds of linen.

Log-wall profiles (see illustration): In addition to being either chinked or scribed, the horizontal wall logs of a log house can be either hewn or left round. Typical combinations include: **A** Chinked two-sided hewn logs stacked vertically, **B** Chinked round logs, **C** Scribed round logs, **D** Chinkless two-sided hewn logs stacked flat, **E** Chinked three-sided hewn logs stacked flat.

Louvre: One of a series of overlapping slats, found in window shutters or doors.

M

Mission style: A late 19th- and early 20th-century functional style, primarily of furniture, in which decoration is mostly confined to emphasis of constructional elements, such as mortise-and-tenon and peg joints. The style evolved from various sources, notably the Shaker communities of North America and the English Arts and Crafts movement. Leading exponents included Gustav Stickley, Frank Lloyd Wright (1869–1959), and Charles and Henry Greene.

Modernism: A style of architecture fashionable from 1920 to the mid-1960s, characterized by asymmetrical compositions, cubic shapes, metal and glass frameworks, large bands of horizontal windows, a flexible arrangement of internal space, and a general absence of mouldings and decorative ornamentation.

Mortise-and-tenon joints: A method of joining two pieces of wood, in which a hole (a mortise) is cut into one piece to house a projection (a tenon) cut into the other piece.

Moulding: Decoratively contoured wood or stone.

Mullion: A vertical bar dividing a window.

N

Neoclassical: A style of architecture and ornamentation that began in the mid-18th century, marked by a return to the repertoire of Graeco-Roman Classicism – loosely in Adam style in Britain and Federal style in the USA, and strictly in the Greek Revival.

Newel post: The post at the end of a staircase, usually attached to both the handrail and the string. On a circular staircase it is the central post around which the stairs curve.

O

Open string: A staircase in which the profile of the treads and risers is visible from the side. The treads support the balustrade.

Oriel window: A bay window on an upper floor.

P

'Painted Lady': A term that originated in the USA and is used to describe 19th-century Victorian houses painted externally in three or more contrasting colours. The architectural styles most commonly associated with this colourful decoration are Italianate, Stick, American Queen Anne and Colonial Revival.

Parquetry: Thin strips of different-coloured hardwoods laid on a sub-floor to form a pattern.

Pendant: An ornament hanging down from a ceiling, staircase, etc.

Pompeiian style: 18th- and 19th-century styles of ornamentation inspired by findings unearthed during the excavation of the ancient Roman city of Pompeii in 1755.

Portico: A roofed porch, often with columns.

Post-and-beam construction: An ancient form of building, in which vertical members support horizontal members.

Post-Modernism: An architectural and design movement that began in the mid-1960s as a reaction against the plain, unadorned forms of Modernism, and looked to traditional and Classical forms, decoration and ornamentation.

Pueblo: Native American communities of the southwest, who live in distinctive flat-roofed houses with walls of adobe and stone.

Purlins: Horizontal timbers in the framework of a roof forming intermediate support for the rafters.

Purlin roof (see illustration): One of the most popular types of roof for log houses, in which the purlins are laid parallel to the ridge log and supported on a number of interior posts and/or load-bearing walls.

Q

Quarries: Small, square- or diamond-shaped panes of glass used in leaded windows.

Quatrefoil: A carved ornament in the form of a four-lobed circle or arch created by cusping.

Queen Anne Revival: The revival began in the 1860s as a reaction to the Gothic Revival and strict Classicism of the early 19th century.

'Queenslander': A style of timber-framed house, prevalent throughout Queensland, Australia. Invariably raised on posts or stumps, it is clad externally and internally with planks, has an iron or tin roof and features a spacious veranda, often embellished with a latticework balustrade.

Quoins: The dressed stones at the corners of a building. They can be simulated in wood.

R

Rafters: Inclined beams supporting a roof covering.

Raftered roof (see illustration): A traditional and popular form of roofing for log houses, in which log rafters run perpendicular to the ridge log.

Log-wall Profiles

A Chinked two-sided hewn logs stacked vertically

B Chinked round logs

C Scribed round logs

D Chinkless two-sided hewn logs stacked flat

E Chinked three-sided hewn logs stacked flat

A   B   C   D   E

Regency style: A style of architecture, decoration, design and furniture popular in England from c. 1810 to the 1830s. Broadly Classical, it drew heavily on French Empire and Etruscan style. However, elements of Greek Revival and Gothic styles were also used, together with Egyptian motifs and Chinoiserie.

Richardsonian-Romanesque style: A large-scale, masculine, Romanesque style of architecture popular in the USA during the late 19th century. It was initiated by Henry Hobson Richardson (1838–86), who had studied at the École des Beaux-Arts in Paris during the early 1860s.

Roof truss: A rigid framework of timbers positioned laterally across a building to carry the longitudinal roof timbers which support the common rafters.

Rosette: Any rose-shaped ornament.

Roundel: A flat ornament or a round window.

S

Santa Fe style: The style of architecture most commonly associated with the southwestern USA and characterized by adobe walls, beamed ceilings, carved wooden doors and sculpted fireplaces. It derives from an eclectic mix of Pueblo, Navaho, Hopi, Zuni, and Spanish and American Colonial styles of architecture and interior decoration.

Sash window: A window formed with sashes – glazed wooden frames that slide up and down in vertical grooves by means of counterbalanced weights. The standard type has two movable sashes and is termed a double-hung sash.

Scandinavian style: A collective term for the various styles of architecture, design and decoration prevalent in Sweden, Norway, Denmark and Finland.

Scribing: Also known as Swedish coping or saddle notching, scribing is a traditional method of stacking logs in a log wall without chinking. Originating in Sweden, the technique involves cutting a U-shaped groove along the underside of a log, into which the round upper side of the underlying log fits snugly.

Shaker style: A style of design, construction and decoration developed by the Shaker communities of North America. Typically, furniture and joinery

made in this style is well made from good-quality timber, usually of simple design in which form follows function.

Shingle: Wooden tiles used to clad exterior walls.

Shingle style: A late 19th-century style of architecture in the USA, which combined wooden shingle cladding, and gambrel and saltbox roofs from the 17th- and early 18th-century houses in New England, with elements of Queen Anne style, such as dormers and oriel windows. In some Shingle-style houses, the woodwork was highly elaborate with patterned shingles, lattices, grilles and balustrading.

Single range: A structure, usually a dwelling, consisting of either one room or a series of connected rooms extending in one direction.

Skip peeling: A method of de-barking logs, in which most of the bark is removed, but some of the outer cambium layers are left intact, resulting in a smooth log with a textured appearance.

Softwood: Timber derived from fast-growing conifer trees, such as pines and firs.

Spanish Colonial Revival: Late 19th- and early 20th-century revival of Spanish Colonial style, which had been imported into the southern and western regions of North America as a result of Spanish colonization during the late 16th century. The revival also reflected elements of simply shaped Pueblo adobe buildings, together with the low, white stucco domestic buildings of the Spanish Mediterranean, and Moorish and Italian Baroque features.

Spindle: A slender rod of wood, thickest in the middle and tapering towards the ends.

Stile: A vertical component of the framework of a door or panelling.

Stick style: Popular type of timber-framed house built in the USA during the late 19th century. Partly derived from balloon-framed buildings, but also from other vernacular styles, such as the Swiss chalet, they are characterized by wide surrounding verandas.

Strapwork: Decoration formed by interlaced strips, either applied or carved in wood, stone or plaster. Often used on ceilings and cornices.

Stave: A bar, rod or staff, usually made of wood.

Stucco: A fine cement or plaster used on the surface of walls, mouldings and other

architectural ornaments. By the 19th century, generally used as a term for exterior rendering.

Studs: The vertical timbers that make up the framework of a wall in a timber-framed building.

T

Thatch: A roof covering made of tightly packed straw or weeds.

Tongue and groove: A method of jointing boards, in which the edge of one board has a tongue that fits into a groove cut into the edge of another.

Transom: The horizontal member across the top or middle of a window or door.

Tread: The horizontal surface of a step.

Truss: A wooden framework in the shape of a large bracket, used to support timbers, such as those in the roof.

Tudor: The period from 1485 to 1603, during which Gothic architecture and ornament was gradually replaced by, or adapted to, classical Renaissance architecture and ornament.

Tudor Revival: A 19th- and 20th-century architectural style that drew on the architecture and the ornamental characteristics and motifs – notably half-timbering, mullions and linenfold panelling – from the Tudor period. Many houses built in this style incorporated Tudor, Elizabethan and Jacobean elements, and were thus loosely described as 'Tudorbethan'.

'Tudorbethan': see Tudor Revival.

V

Veneer: A thin cut of wood (often hardwood) applied as a decorative surface to a lesser piece of wood (often softwood).

Venetian window: A window with a central arched section flanked by two tall, narrow rectangular sections.

Veranda: A roof-covered but otherwise open gallery, porch or balcony supported by posts.

Vernacular architecture: Sometimes referred to as 'architecture without architects', vernacular architecture is generally used to describe houses built in indigenous styles from locally available materials following traditional building practice and patterns.

W

Wainscoting: A simple form of wooden panelling, either full height or on the lower half of a wall.

Wall plate: A timber laid longitudinally on the top of a wall to receive the ends of the rafters. In a timber-framed house the posts and studs of the walls are tenoned into it.

Wattle and daub: A method of wall construction consisting of thin branches or laths, known as wattles, which are fixed in place and roughly plastered over with mud or clay, known as daub. Wattle and daub is often used as a filling between the vertical members of timber-framed houses.

Weatherboards or clapboards: Overlapping wedge-shaped boards forming the external covering of a timber-framed house.

Roof Constructions

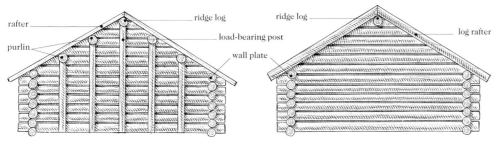

rafter — ridge log
purlin — load-bearing post
wall plate

ridge log
log rafter

Purlin Roof

Raftered Roof

Index

Acknowledgements

The author and publisher would like to thank the following people for their invaluable help in the preparation of this book.

Rodney Archer
Donna Baron
Jonathan and Pauline Barres
Marina and Bill Beadleston
Peter Beale
Dr Tom and Mrs Pat Bell
Don and Anne Cameron
Frank and Suz Cameron
Cathy Capri
Simon and Robyn Carnachan
Jim and Hilda Chapman
Patrick Cooke
Carolyn Davies
Ischa van Delft
Sherri Donghia and Roger Eulau
Priscilla Endicott
Dave Fritchley
Kevin and Sue Godley
Olav Golid
Jolie and Petrea Grant
Isak I Grave
Annie Har and William Hayes
Sue and Dick Hare
Happy Hawn
Astrid Poulsson Hesledalen
Hallgrim Høydal
Jon Geir and Inger Høyersten
Angela Kent
Richard Lewis and Donna Allen
Christian Liaigre
Holly Lueders and Richard Spizzirri
Rob and Sarah McConnell
Stephen P Mack
John Mainwaring
Alf and Wendy Martensson
Graham Moss
Bergit Myrjord
Gerallt D Nash
Chris Ohrstrom
Marilyn Phipps
Alan and Marion Powell
Mark Pynn
Michèle Rédélé
Anna and Halvor Rekaa
Margaret Rogers
Jim Ruscitto
Allan Shope
Jocelyne and Jean Louis Sibuet
Philip and Barbara Silver
Jørgen H Sønstebø
Tone Stivi
Kare Sveen
Tony Suttle
Olivier Vidal

Credits

The following abbreviations have been used:

T Top
B Bottom
L Left
R Right
C Centre

Athelhampton House
Athelhampton
Dorchester
Dorset DT2 7LG
England
pp. 11BR, 91, 92–3, 144R, 169R, 183TL and TR

The Buttolph Williams House
249 Broad Street
Wethersfield
CT 06109
USA
pp. 47, 140TL, 148TR

Glomdalsmuseet
Museum for Østerdalen and Solor
2400 Elverum
Norway
pp. 23BR, 24–5, 100–1, 159TR

Heddal-og Nottodden Museum
Bygdetunet
Heddal
Norway
pp. 168L, 178–9

The Hempstead House
11 Hempstead Street
New London
CT 06320
USA
pp. 46BL and BR, 148TL

Hotel Mont-Blanc
Place de l'Église;
Les Fermes de Marie
Chemin de Riante Colline;
Les Fermes des Grand Champ
Choseaux
74120 Megève
France
pp. 20TR, 21TR, 22, 72–3, 103BL and BR, 161C, BL and BR, 181BL and BR

Museum of Welsh Life
St Fagan's
Cardiff CF5 6XB
Wales
pp. 32–3, 34B, 35B, 66R, 130

The National Trust Queensland
Old Government House
George Street
Brisbane 4000
Queensland
Australia
Bellevue Homestead, Coominya: *pp. 1, 103TL and TR, 114T, 115, 168R, 170TR, 171BC*
Mayes Cottage, Logan (managed by Logan City Council): *p. 170TL*

Roseland Cottage
204 Roseland Parkroad
Woodstock
CT 06281
USA
(run by S.P.N.E.A.) *p. 52BR*

Ellen Terry Museum
Smallhythe Place
Smallhythe
Nr Tenterden
Kent TN30 7NG
England
p. 35T

The Webb-Deane-Stevens Museum
211 Main Street
Wethersfield
CT 06109
USA
pp. 2, 46TL and TR, 49T and BR, 94T and BR, 95T, 131B, 140BL and BR, 147BL, 149TL and BL, 154L, TR and BR, 155B, 162TL, 163TR and BR, 172L and C, 183BL

Grateful thanks to the following architectural, building and interior design companies whose houses and work has been photographed:

Simon Carnachan
Carnachan Architects Ltd
(Architects, interior designers and landscape architects)
27 Bath Street
Parnell
PO Box 37-717
Auckland
New Zealand
pp. 3, 62BL–R, 124–5

Conger Fuller Architects
710 East Durant Street
Aspen
CO 81611
USA
pp. 8–9, 18, 67R, 89, 138TL and TC, 153TR

Ischa van Delft
(Interior decorator)
September
Vughterstraat 72
5211 GK's-Hertogenbosch
Holland
pp. 114BL–R, 133BL, 137L, 144TL, 154C, 162R

Donghia Furniture/Textiles
485 Broadway
New York
NY 10013
USA
pp. 4–5, 13TL, 56–7, 64–5, 67L, 118TC and B, 135L and B, 155TL, 160TL, 164L, 165TL, 180

Annie Har
Sunnit Architects
10 Attunga Lane
Mount Glorious
Queensland 4520
Australia
p. 102R

Angela Kent
(Architect)
Kenström Design Pty Ltd
92 Cathedral Street
Woolloomooloo
NSW 2011
Australia
pp. 13BR, 14–15, 122–3, 137B

Christian Liaigre
(Furniture and interior designer)
Bureau d'Études
122 rue de Grenelle
75007 Paris
France
pp. 116, 117T, 133R, 134BR, 141BR, 145BR, 156BR, 157TR, 159BR, 161TR and CR

Holly Lueders Design
(Building, interior and furniture design)
27 West 67 Street
New York
NY 10023
USA
pp. 7, 11TR, 17R, 28–9, 78–81, 129L, 138R, 158TR and BR, 159L, 161L, 164R, 165C

Rob and Sarah McConnell
(Builder and paint specialist)
8 Coastguard Cottages
Coastguard Square
Rye Harbour
East Sussex TN31 7TS
England; in conjunction with
Dave Fritchley
(Log detailing/twig work and rustic furniture specialist)
Eggshole Cottage
Starvecrow Lane
Peasmarsh
East Sussex TN3 16XN
pp. 11BL, 30–1, 106–7

Stephen P Mack
(A nationally renowned designer and expert in the restoration and reconstruction of 17th- and 18th-century structures and their environs)
Stephen P Mack Associates
Chase Hill Farm
Ashaway
RI 02804
USA
Home of Stephen P Mack:
pp. 48T and BR, 49BL, 136, 140TR, 142TR, 143BR, 147TL and TR, 148B, 156T and BC, 169L, 171TR, 174BL and BC
Work of Stephen P Mack:
pp. 16R–17L, 50–1, 90, 94BL, 131TL, 142BL–R, 144BL, 146T and BR, 147BR, 172TR, 174TL and TR, 181BR, 183BR

John Mainwaring & Associates Pty Ltd
(Architects and urban designers)
PO Box 958
Noosa Heads
Queensland 4567
Australia
pp. 62T, 63, 129R, 152BL–R, 153L and BR, 171BL

Graham Moss
(Specialist conservator of early buildings, architectural, constructional and decorative finishes.)
Moss Co Architects
Brookgate
Plealey
Shrewsbury SY5 0UY
England
pp. 38TR and BR, 40, 74–5, 102L, 142TL and TC, 143TR, 177T, 181TR

Chris Ohrstrom
Historic Paints Ltd
Burr Tavern
Route 1, PO Box 474
East Meredith
New York
NY 13757
USA
pp. 42–3, 95B, 134L, 141BL, 143L, 145BL, 146BL, 149TR, 156L, 157BR, 162BL, 163L, 170BL and BC, 173B, 174BR

Mark Pynn
(Architect)
Darryl Charles McMillen
Box 1068
Sun Valley
ID 83353
USA
pp. 58–9, 132, 133TL, 140TC, 160BL

Michèle Rédélé
(Interior designer)
90 Boulevard Malegerbes
Paris 75008
France
pp. 21TL, 68–71, 131R, 160R, 181TL

Jim Ruscitto
(Architect)
Ruscitto, Latham, Blanton
PO Box 419
Sun Valley
ID 83353
USA
pp. 13TR, 26–7, 82–8, 126–7, 128L, 152T, 158L, CT and CB, 165BL and BR

Allan Shope
(Architect)
Shope, Reno, Wharton Associates
18 West Putnam Avenue
Greenwich
CT 06830
USA
pp. 66L, 108–9, 128R, 138BL and BC

Tony Suttle
Woods Bagot Pty Ltd
Architects
64 Marine Parade
Southport
Queensland 4215
Australia
pp. 61, 119, 170BR

Olivier Vidal and Associates
(Architects)
14 rue Moncey
75009 Paris
France
pp. 11TL, 120–1, 141TL–R

The author would like to thank Zia Mattocks, Paul Tilby, Sian Parkhouse, Cathy Ebbels and Nadine Bazar for all their invaluable hard work, diligence and enthusiasm.